2012-2013 Supplement

National Security Law
Fifth Edition

and

Counterterrorism Law
Second Edition

2012-2013 Supplement

National Security Law
Fifth Edition

and

Counterterrorism Law
Second Edition

Stephen Dycus
Professor of Law
Vermont Law School

William C. Banks
Board of Advisors Distinguished Professor
Syracuse University

Peter Raven-Hansen
Glen Earl Weston Research Professor of Law
George Washington University

Stephen I. Vladeck
Professor of Law
American University Washington College of Law

Wolters Kluwer
Law & Business

Published by Wolters Kluwer Law & Business in New York.

Wolters Kluwer Law & Business serves customers worldwide with CCH, Aspen Publishers, and Kluwer Law International products. (www.wolterskluwerlb.com)

To contact Customer Service, e-mail customer.service@wolterskluwer.com, call 1-800-234-1660, fax 1-800-901-9075, or mail correspondence to:

Wolters Kluwer Law & Business
Attn: Order Department
PO Box 990
Frederick, MD 21705

Printed in the United States of America.

1234567890

ISBN: 978-1-4548-2539-5

Certified Chain of Custody
Product Line Contains At Least
20% Certified Forest Content
www.sfiprogram.org
SFI-00756

About Wolters Kluwer Law & Business

Wolters Kluwer Law & Business is a leading global provider of intelligent information and digital solutions for legal and business professionals in key specialty areas, and respected educational resources for professors and law students. Wolters Kluwer Law & Business connects legal and business professionals as well as those in the education market with timely, specialized authoritative content and information-enabled solutions to support success through productivity, accuracy and mobility.

Serving customers worldwide, Wolters Kluwer Law & Business products include those under the Aspen Publishers, CCH, Kluwer Law International, Loislaw, Best Case, ftwilliam.com and MediRegs family of products.

CCH products have been a trusted resource since 1913, and are highly regarded resources for legal, securities, antitrust and trade regulation, government contracting, banking, pension, payroll, employment and labor, and healthcare reimbursement and compliance professionals.

Aspen Publishers products provide essential information to attorneys, business professionals and law students. Written by preeminent authorities, the product line offers analytical and practical information in a range of specialty practice areas from securities law and intellectual property to mergers and acquisitions and pension/benefits. Aspen's trusted legal education resources provide professors and students with high-quality, up-to-date and effective resources for successful instruction and study in all areas of the law.

Kluwer Law International products provide the global business community with reliable international legal information in English. Legal practitioners, corporate counsel and business executives around the world rely on Kluwer Law journals, looseleafs, books, and electronic products for comprehensive information in many areas of international legal practice.

Loislaw is a comprehensive online legal research product providing legal content to law firm practitioners of various specializations. Loislaw provides attorneys with the ability to quickly and efficiently find the necessary legal information they need, when and where they need it, by facilitating access to primary law as well as state-specific law, records, forms and treatises.

Best Case Solutions is the leading bankruptcy software product to the bankruptcy industry. It provides software and workflow tools to flawlessly streamline petition preparation and the electronic filing process, while timely incorporating ever-changing court requirements.

ftwilliam.com offers employee benefits professionals the highest quality plan documents (retirement, welfare and non-qualified) and government forms (5500/PBGC, 1099 and IRS) software at highly competitive prices.

MediRegs products provide integrated health care compliance content and software solutions for professionals in healthcare, higher education and life sciences, including professionals in accounting, law and consulting.

Wolters Kluwer Law & Business, a division of Wolters Kluwer, is headquartered in New York. Wolters Kluwer is a market-leading global information services company focused on professionals.

Contents

Preface

The Fifth Edition of *National Security Law* has been in print for less than a year as this is written, the Second Edition of *Counterterrorism Law* only a few months. Yet the pace of important developments in the field continues at such a rapid clip that this *Supplement* is already needed to provide updates.

We regard the dynamic quality of our subject as one of its chief attractions. But that same quality presents challenges for students and teachers alike. In our classes we stress the currency and practical relevance of these materials by discussing events in the news every day. In the process, we gain a special insight into the workings of law and government, and into the responsibility of lawyers to help keep us safe and free.

This year's *Supplement* includes a report from President Obama on the deployment of U.S. troops around the world, a statement by John Brennan on U.S. counterterrorism strategy, and remarks by Attorney General Holder about targeted killing and military commissions. Also included here are a new ODNI procedure for notifying the intelligence committees of non-covert activities, and DNI guidelines for NCTC access, use, and retention of personal data held by other agencies. New legislation authorizing military detention of terrorist suspects is followed by a presidential signing statement, a directive for implementing one part of the law, and a district court ruling that another part of the law is unconstitutional. Finally, this *Supplement* includes recent decisions in cases involving government watchlists, the personal liability of a government lawyer for advice authorizing torture, and jurisdiction to consider the personal liability of other government officials for mistreatment of terrorist suspects imprisoned at Guantánamo.

This *Supplement* serves two closely related casebooks: *National Security Law (5th ed.)* and *Counterterrorism Law (2d ed.)*. This Preface is followed immediately by two Teacher's Guides, one for each book, which indicate the placement of supplemental materials in each casebook. Each document listed is accompanied by a reference to one or both casebooks. For example, the decision in *Al-Zahrani v. Rodriguez* appears with this instruction: **[NSL p. 810, CTL p. 424. Insert after the *Rasul* decision.]**. "NSL" refers to *National Security Law (5th ed.)*, "CTL" to *Counterterrorism Law (2d ed.)*.

As important new developments arise, we will continue to document them by posting edited new materials on the websites for the two casebooks, from which they may be downloaded by teachers and shared with students. The website for *National Security Law (5th ed.)* is at http://www.aspenlawschool.com/books/dycus_nationalsecurity/; for *Counterterrorism Law (2d ed.)* at http://www.aspenlawschool.com/ books/ dycus_counterterrorism/.

With this Supplement we are very pleased to welcome Professor Stephen I. Vladeck of American University's Washington College of Law to our project. As always, we are extremely grateful to our adopters, fellow members of the National Security Law Section of the Association of American Law Schools, fellow members of the Editorial Board of the *Journal of National Security Law & Policy*, fellow casebook authors (our collaborators in building the field), and our many friends in the national security community. We also wish to thank our research assistants: Jason Thelen at American University Washington College of Law and Alexander Mullee at Vermont Law School. Finally, we are grateful to John Devins, Eric Holt, Barbara Roth, and Carol McGeehan of Aspen Publishers for their continued encouragement and support.

Stephen Dycus
William C. Banks
Peter Raven-Hansen
Stephen I. Vladeck

June 2012

Teacher's Guide for
National Security Law
(5th Edition)

Chapter 20. The Fourth Amendment and National Security

Chapter 21. Congressional Authority for Foreign Intelligence Surveillance

Chapter 22. Programmatic Electronic Surveillance for Foreign Intelligence

Chapter 23. Third-Party Records and Data Mining

Chapter 24. Screening for Security

Chapter 28. The Great Writ: Habeas Corpus After 9/11

Chapter 30. Military Detention After 9/11

Chapter 32. Case Study: Coercive Interrogation by U.S. Forces After 9/11

Chapter 36. Trial by Military Commission

* * *

Teacher's Guide for Counterterrorism Law (2d Edition)

Chapter 16. Military Detention After 9/11

Chapter 18. Case Study: Coercive Interrogation by U.S. Forces After 9/11

Chapter 22. Trial by Military Commission

* * *

Table of Cases

* * *

Presidential Letter — 2012 War Powers Resolution 6-Month Report

June 15, 2012

Dear Mr. Speaker: (Dear Mr. President:)

I am providing this supplemental consolidated report, prepared by my Administration and consistent with the War Powers Resolution (Public Law 93-148), as part of my efforts to keep the Congress informed about deployments of U.S. Armed Forces equipped for combat.

MILITARY OPERATIONS AGAINST AL-QA'IDA, THE TALIBAN, AND ASSOCIATED FORCES AND IN SUPPORT OF RELATED U.S. COUNTERTERRORISM (CT) OBJECTIVES

Since October 7, 2001, the United States has conducted combat operations in Afghanistan against al-Qa'ida terrorists, their Taliban supporters, and associated forces. In support of these and other overseas operations, the United States has deployed combat equipped forces to a number of locations in the U.S. Central, Pacific, European, Southern, and Africa Command areas of operation. Previously such operations and deployments have been reported, consistent with Public Law 107-40 and the War Powers Resolution, and operations and deployments remain ongoing. These operations, which the United States has carried out with the assistance of numerous international partners, have degraded al-Qa'ida's capabilities and brought an end to the Taliban's leadership of Afghanistan.

United States Armed Forces are now actively pursuing and engaging remaining al-Qa'ida and Taliban fighters in Afghanistan. The total number of U.S. forces in Afghanistan is approximately 90,000, of which more than 70,000 are assigned to the North Atlantic Treaty Organization (NATO)-led International Security Assistance Force (ISAF) in Afghanistan. In accordance with June 2011 Presidential guidance, the Department of Defense remains on track to achieve a Force Management Level of 68,000 U.S. forces by the end of this summer. After that, reductions will continue at a steady pace.

The U.N. Security Council most recently reaffirmed its authorization

1

of ISAF for a 12-month period until October 13, 2012, in U.N. Security Council Resolution 2011 (October 12, 2011). The mission of ISAF, under NATO command and in partnership with the Government of the Islamic Republic of Afghanistan, is to prevent Afghanistan from once again becoming a safe haven for international terrorists. . . .

United States Armed Forces are detaining in Afghanistan approximately 2,748 individuals under the Authorization for the Use of Military Force (Public Law 107-40) as informed by the laws of war. . . .

The combat-equipped forces, deployed since January 2002 to Naval Base, Guantanamo Bay, Cuba, continue to conduct secure detention operations for the approximately 169 detainees at Guantanamo Bay under Public Law 107-40 and consistent with principles of the law of war.

In furtherance of U.S. efforts against members of al-Qa'ida, the Taliban, and associated forces, the United States continues to work with partners around the globe . . . .

In . . . a limited number of cases, the U.S. military has taken direct action in Somalia against members of al-Qa'ida, including those who are also members of al-Shabaab, who are engaged in efforts to carry out terrorist attacks against the United States and our interests.

The U.S. military has also been working closely with the Yemeni government to operationally dismantle and ultimately eliminate the terrorist threat posed by al-Qa'ida in the Arabian Peninsula (AQAP), the most active and dangerous affiliate of al-Qa'ida today. Our joint efforts have resulted in direct action against a limited number of AQAP operatives and senior leaders in that country who posed a terrorist threat to the United States and our interests.

. . . As necessary, in response to the terrorist threat, I will direct additional measures against al-Qa'ida, the Taliban, and associated forces to protect U.S. citizens and interests. It is not possible to know at this time the precise scope or the duration of the deployments of U.S. Armed Forces necessary to counter this terrorist threat to the United States. A classified annex to this report provides further information.

MILITARY OPERATIONS IN IRAQ

The United States completed its responsible withdrawal of U.S. forces from Iraq in December 2011, in accordance with the 2008 Agreement Between the United States of America and the Republic of Iraq on the Withdrawal of United States Forces from Iraq and the

Organization of Their Activities during Their Temporary Presence in Iraq.

MILITARY OPERATIONS IN CENTRAL AFRICA

In October and November 2011, U.S. military personnel with appropriate combat equipment deployed to Uganda to serve as advisors to regional forces that are working to apprehend or remove Joseph Kony and other senior Lord's Resistance Army (LRA) leaders from the battlefield, and to protect local populations. The total number of U.S. military personnel deployed for this mission, including those providing logistical and support functions, is approximately 90. United States forces are working with select partner nation forces to enhance cooperation, information-sharing and synchronization, operational planning, and overall effectiveness. Elements of these U.S. forces have deployed to forward locations in the LRA-affected areas of the Republic of South Sudan, the Democratic Republic of the Congo, and the Central African Republic to enhance regional efforts against the LRA. These forces, however, will not engage LRA forces except in self-defense. It is in the U.S. national security interest to help our regional partners in Africa to develop their capability to address threats to regional peace and security, including the threat posed by the LRA. . . .

MARITIME INTERCEPTION OPERATIONS

As noted in previous reports, the United States remains prepared to conduct maritime interception operations on the high seas in the areas of responsibility of each of the geographic combatant commands. These maritime operations are aimed at stopping the movement, arming, and financing of certain international terrorist groups, and also include operations aimed at stopping proliferation by sea of weapons of mass destruction and related materials. Additional information is provided in the classified annex.

HOSTAGE RESCUE OPERATIONS

. . . [O]n January 24, 2012, U.S. Special Operations Forces conducted a successful operation in Somalia to rescue Ms. Jessica Buchanan, a U.S. citizen who had been kidnapped by individuals linked to Somali pirate groups and financiers.

MILITARY OPERATIONS IN EGYPT

Approximately 693 military personnel are assigned to the U.S. contingent of the Multinational Force and Observers, which have been present in Egypt since 1981.

U.S.-NATO OPERATIONS IN KOSOVO

The U.N. Security Council authorized Member States to establish a NATO-led Kosovo Force (KFOR) in Resolution 1244 on June 10, 1999. The original mission of KFOR was to monitor, verify, and, when necessary, enforce compliance with the Military Technical Agreement between NATO and the then-Federal Republic of Yugoslavia (now Serbia), while maintaining a safe and secure environment. Today, KFOR deters renewed hostilities in cooperation with local authorities, bilateral partners, and international institutions. The principal military tasks of KFOR forces are to help maintain a safe and secure environment and to ensure freedom of movement throughout Kosovo.

Currently, 23 NATO Allies contribute to KFOR. Seven non-NATO countries also participate. The United States contribution to KFOR is approximately 817 U.S. military personnel out of the total strength of approximately 6,401 personnel . . . .

I have directed the participation of U.S. Armed Forces in all of these operations pursuant to my constitutional and statutory authority as Commander in Chief (including the authority to carry out Public Law 107-40 and other statutes) and as Chief Executive, as well as my constitutional and statutory authority to conduct the foreign relations of the United States. Officials of my Administration and I communicate regularly with the leadership and other Members of Congress with regard to these deployments, and we will continue to do so.

Barack Obama

[NSL p. 403, CTL p. 117. Insert after Note 7.]

John O. Brennan, Assistant to the President for Homeland Security and Counterterrorism, The Efficacy and Ethics of the President's Counterterrorism Strategy

Remarks at the Woodrow Wilson Int'l Center for Scholars, Apr. 30, 2012
available at http://www.wilsoncenter.org/event/the-efficacy-and-ethics-us-counterterrorism-strategy

. . .

This leads me to the final point I want to discuss today, the rigorous standards and process of review to which we hold ourselves today when considering and authorizing strikes against a specific member of al-Qaida outside the hot battlefield of Afghanistan. What I hope to do is to give you a general sense, in broad terms, of the high bar we require ourselves to meet when making these profound decisions today. That includes not only whether a specific member of al-Qaida can legally be pursued with lethal force, but also whether he should be.

Over time, we've worked to refine, clarify, and strengthen this process and our standards, and we continue to do so. If our counterterrorism professionals assess, for example, that a suspected member of al-Qaida poses such a threat to the United States to warrant lethal action, they may raise that individual's name for consideration. The proposal will go through a careful review and, as appropriate, will be evaluated by the very most senior officials in our government for a decision.

First and foremost, the individual must be a legitimate target under the law. Earlier, I described how the use of force against members of al-Qaida is authorized under both international and U.S. law, including both the inherent right of national self-defense and the 2001 Authorization for Use of Military Force, which courts have held extends to those who are part of al-Qaida, the Taliban, and associated forces. If, after a legal review, we determine that the individual is not a lawful target, end of discussion. We are a nation of laws, and we will always act within the bounds of the law.

Of course, the law only establishes the outer limits of the authority in which counterterrorism professionals can operate. Even if we determine that it is lawful to pursue the terrorist in question with lethal force, it doesn't necessarily mean we should. There are, after all, literally thousands of individuals who are part of al-Qaida, the Taliban, or associated forces, thousands upon thousands. Even if it were possible, going after every single one of these individuals with lethal force would neither be wise nor an effective use of our intelligence and counterterrorism resources.

As a result, we have to be strategic. Even if it is lawful to pursue a specific member of al-Qaida, we ask ourselves whether that individual's activities rise to a certain threshold for action, and whether taking action will, in fact, enhance our security.

For example, when considering lethal force we ask ourselves whether the individual poses a significant threat to U.S. interests. This is absolutely critical, and it goes to the very essence of why we take this kind of exceptional action. We do not engage in legal action — in lethal action in order to eliminate every single member of al-Qaida in the world. Most times, and as we have done for more than a decade, we rely on cooperation with other countries that are also interested in removing these terrorists with their own capabilities and within their own laws. Nor is lethal action about punishing terrorists for past crimes; we are not seeking vengeance. Rather, we conduct targeted strikes because they are necessary to mitigate an actual ongoing threat, to stop plots, prevent future attacks, and to save American lives.

And what do we mean when we say significant threat? I am not referring to some hypothetical threat, the mere possibility that a member of al-Qaida might try to attack us at some point in the future. A significant threat might be posed by an individual who is an operational leader of al-Qaida or one of its associated forces. Or perhaps the individual is himself an operative, in the midst of actually training for or planning to carry out attacks against U.S. persons and interests. Or perhaps the individual possesses unique operational skills that are being leveraged in a planned attack. The purpose of a strike against a particular individual is to stop him before he can carry out his attack and kill innocents. The purpose is to disrupt his plans and his plots before they come to fruition.

In addition, our unqualified preference is to only undertake lethal force when we believe that capturing the individual is not feasible. I have heard it suggested that the Obama Administration somehow prefers killing al-Qaida members rather than capturing them. Nothing could be further from the truth. It is our preference to capture suspected terrorists whenever and wherever feasible.

For one reason, this allows us to gather valuable intelligence that we might not be able to obtain any other way. In fact, the members of al-Qaida that we or other nations have captured have been one of our greatest sources of information about al-Qaida, its plans, and its intentions. And once in U.S. custody, we often can prosecute them in our federal courts or reformed military commissions, both of which are used for gathering intelligence and preventing future terrorist attacks.

You see our preference for capture in the case of Ahmed Warsame, a member of al-Shabaab who had significant ties to al-Qaida in the Arabian Peninsula. Last year, when we learned that he would be traveling from Yemen to Somalia, U.S. forces captured him in route and we subsequently charged him in federal court.

The reality, however, is that since 2001 such unilateral captures by U.S. forces outside of hot battlefields, like Afghanistan, have been exceedingly rare. This is due in part to the fact that in many parts of the world our counterterrorism partners have been able to capture or kill dangerous individuals themselves.

Moreover, after being subjected to more than a decade of relentless pressure, al-Qaida's ranks have dwindled and scattered. These terrorists are skilled at seeking remote, inhospitable terrain, places where the United States and our partners simply do not have the ability to arrest or capture them. At other times, our forces might have the ability to attempt capture, but only by putting the lives of our personnel at too great a risk. Oftentimes, attempting capture could subject civilians to unacceptable risks. There are many reasons why capture might not be feasible, in which case lethal force might be the only remaining option to address the threat, prevent an attack, and save lives.

Finally, when considering lethal force we are of course mindful that there are important checks on our ability to act unilaterally in foreign territories. We do not use force whenever we want, wherever we want. International legal principles, including respect for a state's sovereignty and the laws of war, impose constraints. The United States of America respects national sovereignty and international law. . . .

As President Obama's counterterrorism advisor, I feel that it is important for the American people to know that these efforts are overseen with extraordinary care and thoughtfulness. The president expects us to address all of the tough questions I have discussed today. Is capture really not feasible? Is this individual a significant threat to U.S. interests? Is this really the best option? Have we thought through the consequences, especially any unintended ones? Is this really going to help protect our country from further attacks? Is this going to save lives?

Our commitment to upholding the ethics and efficacy of this counterterrorism tool continues even after we decide to pursue a specific terrorist in this way. For example, we only authorize a particular operation against a specific individual if we have a high degree of confidence that the individual being targeted is indeed the terrorist we are pursuing. This is a very high bar. Of course, how we identify an individual naturally involves intelligence sources and methods, which I will not discuss. Suffice it to say, our intelligence community has multiple ways to determine, with a high degree of confidence, that the individual being targeted is indeed the al-Qaida terrorist we are seeking.

In addition, we only authorize a strike if we have a high degree of confidence that innocent civilians will not be injured or killed, except in the rarest of circumstances. The unprecedented advances we have made in technology provide us greater proximity to target[s] for a longer period of time, and as a result allow us to better understand what is happening in real time on the ground in ways that were previously impossible. We can be much more discriminating and we can make more informed judgments about factors that might contribute to collateral damage.

I can tell you today that there have indeed been occasions when we decided against conducting a strike in order to avoid the injury or death of innocent civilians. This reflects our commitment to doing everything in our power to avoid civilian casualties, even if it means having to come back another day to take out that terrorist, as we have done previously. And I would note that these standards, for identifying a target and avoiding the . . . loss of lives of innocent civilians, exceed what is required as a matter of international law on a typical battlefield. That's another example of the high standards to which we hold ourselves.

Our commitment to ensuring accuracy and effectiveness continues even after a strike. In the wake of a strike, we harness the full range of our intelligence capabilities to assess whether the mission in fact achieved its objective. We try to determine whether there was any collateral damage, including civilian deaths. There is, of course, no such thing as a perfect weapon, and remotely piloted aircraft are no exception.

As the president and others have acknowledged, there have indeed been instances when, despite the extraordinary precautions we take, civilians have been accidently . . . injured, or worse, killed in these strikes. It is exceedingly rare, but it has happened. When it does, it pains us, and we regret it deeply, as we do any time innocents are killed in war. And when it happens we take it very, very seriously. We go back and we review our actions. We examine our practices. And we constantly work to improve and refine our efforts so that we are doing everything in our power to prevent the loss of innocent life. This too is a reflection of our values as Americans.

Ensuring the ethics and efficacy of these strikes also includes regularly informing appropriate members of Congress and the committees who have oversight of our counterterrorism programs. Indeed, our counterterrorism programs, including the use of lethal force, have grown more effective over time because of congressional oversight and our ongoing dialogue with members and staff. . . .

[NSL p. 410, CTL p. 124. Insert at end of chapter.]

6. *Targeted Killing of U.S. Citizens?*

Eric Holder, Attorney General, Remarks at Northwestern University School of Law

Mar. 5, 2012,
available at
http://www.justice.gov/iso/opa/ag/speeches/2012/ag-speech-1203051.html

. . .

Now, it is an unfortunate but undeniable fact that some of the threats we face come from a small number of United States citizens who have decided to commit violent attacks against their own country from abroad. Based on generations-old legal principles and Supreme Court decisions handed down during World War II, as well as during this current conflict, it's clear that United States citizenship alone does not make such individuals immune from being targeted. But it does mean that the government must take into account all relevant constitutional considerations with respect to United States citizens — even those who are leading efforts to kill innocent Americans. Of these, the most relevant is the Fifth Amendment's Due Process Clause, which says that the government may not deprive a citizen of his or her life without due process of law.

The Supreme Court has made clear that the Due Process Clause does not impose one-size-fits-all requirements, but instead mandates procedural safeguards that depend on specific circumstances. In cases arising under the Due Process Clause — including in a case involving a U.S. citizen captured in the conflict against al Qaeda — the Court has applied a balancing approach, weighing the private interest that will be affected against the interest the government is trying to protect, and the burdens the government would face in providing additional process. Where national security operations are at stake, due process takes into account the realities of combat.

Here, the interests on both sides of the scale are extraordinarily weighty. An individual's interest in making sure that the government does not target him erroneously could not be more significant. Yet it is imperative for the government to counter threats posed by senior operational leaders of al Qaeda, and to protect the innocent people whose lives could be lost in their attacks.

Any decision to use lethal force against a United States citizen — even one intent on murdering Americans and who has become an operational leader of al-Qaeda in a foreign land — is among the gravest that government leaders can face. The American people can be — and deserve to be — assured that actions taken in their defense are consistent with their values and their laws. So, although I cannot discuss or confirm any particular program or operation, I believe it is important to explain these legal principles publicly.

Let me be clear: an operation using lethal force in a foreign country, targeted against a U.S. citizen who is a senior operational leader of al Qaeda or associated forces, and who is actively engaged in planning to kill Americans, would be lawful at least in the following circumstances: First, the U.S. government has determined, after a thorough and careful review, that the individual poses an imminent threat of violent attack against the United States; second, capture is not feasible; and third, the operation would be conducted in a manner consistent with applicable law of war principles.

The evaluation of whether an individual presents an "imminent threat" incorporates considerations of the relevant window of opportunity to act, the possible harm that missing the window would cause to civilians, and the likelihood of heading off future disastrous attacks against the United States. As we learned on 9/11, al Qaeda has demonstrated the ability to strike with little or no notice — and to cause devastating casualties. Its leaders are continually planning attacks against the United States, and they do not behave like a traditional military — wearing uniforms, carrying arms openly, or massing forces in preparation for an attack. Given these facts, the Constitution does not require the President to delay action until some theoretical end-stage of planning — when the precise time, place, and manner of an attack become clear. Such a requirement would create an unacceptably high risk that our efforts would fail, and that Americans would be killed.

Whether the capture of a U.S. citizen terrorist is feasible is a fact-specific, and potentially time-sensitive, question. It may depend on, among other things, whether capture can be accomplished in the window of time available to prevent an attack and without undue risk to civilians or to U.S. personnel. Given the nature of how terrorists act and where they tend to hide, it may not always be feasible to capture a United States citizen terrorist who presents an imminent threat of violent attack. In that case, our government has the clear authority to defend the United States with lethal force. . . .

[NSL p. 464. Insert after Note 2.]

In November 2011, Director of National Intelligence James Clapper issued an Intelligence Community Directive that elaborates on reporting required by statute to keep the congressional intelligence committees "fully and currently informed of the intelligence activities of the United States" (see p. 504). The Directive adds to statutory obligations by requiring agencies of the Intelligence Community to report in writing, to report on intelligence failures, and to resolve any doubts in favor of reporting. But it does not apply to separately prescribed reporting of covert actions (see p. 505).

Office of the Director of National Intelligence, Intelligence Community Directive Number 112: Congressional Notification
Nov. 16, 2011
http://www.dni.gov/electronic_reading_room/ICD_112.pdf

C. APPLICABILITY . . .

3. This Directive does not apply to reporting of covert actions to the Congressional intelligence committees, to statutory reporting

requirements for IC Inspectors General, or to routine informational briefings.

D. POLICY . . .

2. The provisions of this Directive shall be interpreted with a presumption of notification in fulfillment of the statutory requirement to keep the Congressional intelligence committees fully and currently informed of all intelligence activities.

3. It is IC policy that IC elements shall, in a timely manner, keep the Congressional intelligence committees fully informed, in writing, of all significant anticipated intelligence activities, significant intelligence failures, significant intelligence activities, and illegal activities. . . .

5. Determining whether written notification should be provided of a particular intelligence activity is a judgment based on all the facts and circumstances known to the IC element, and on the nature and extent of previous notifications or briefings to Congress on the same matter. Not every intelligence activity warrants written notification. Facts and circumstances of intelligence activities change over time; therefore, IC elements must continually assess whether there is an obligation to report a matter pursuant to the National Security Act and this Directive.

6. As required by the National Security Act, Congress must receive written notification of significant anticipated intelligence activities and significant intelligence failures. General guidelines for determining the types of intelligence activities that warrant written notification follow:
    a. Significant anticipated intelligence activities include:
      (1) intelligence activities that entail, with reasonable foreseeability, significant risk of exposure, compromise, and loss of human life;
      (2) intelligence activities that are expected to have a major impact on important foreign policy or national security interests;
      (3) an IC element's transfer, to a recipient outside that IC element, of defense articles, personnel services, or "controlled equipment" valued in excess of $1 million as provided in Section 505 of the National Security Act;
      (4) extensive organizational changes in an IC element;
      (5) deployment of new collection techniques that represent a

significant departure from previous operations or activities or that result from evidence of significant foreign developments;

(6) significant activities undertaken pursuant to specific direction of the President or the National Security Council (this is not applicable to covert action, which is covered by Section 503 of the National Security Act); or

(7) significant acquisition, reprogramming, or non-routine budgetary actions that are of Congressional concern and that are not otherwise reportable under the National Intelligence Program Procedures for Reprogramming and Transfers.

b. Significant intelligence failures are failures that are extensive in scope, continuing in nature, or likely to have a serious impact on United States (US) national security interests and include:

(1) the loss or compromise of classified information on such a scale or over such an extended period as to indicate a systemic loss or compromise of classified intelligence information that may pose a substantial risk to US national security interests;

(2) a significant unauthorized disclosure of classified intelligence infonnation that may pose a substantial risk to US national security interests;

(3) a potentially pervasive failure, interruption, or compromise of a collection capability or collection system; or

(4) a conclusion that an intelligence product is the result of foreign deception or denial activity, or otherwise contains major errors in analysis, with a significant impact on US national security policies, programs, or activities.

7. As a matter of policy, IC elements shall provide Congress written notification of other significant intelligence activities and illegal activities. General guidelines for determining these types of intelligence activities warranting notification follow.

a. Significant intelligence activities include:

(1) substantial changes in the capabilities or known vulnerabilities of US intelligence operations or intelligence systems or resources;

(2) programmatic developments likely to be of Congressional interest, such as major cost overruns, a major modification of, or the termination of a significant contract;

(3) developments that affect intelligence programs, projects, or activities that are likely to be of Congressional concern

because of their substantial impact on national security or
foreign policy;

(4) the loss of life in the performance of an intelligence
activity; or

(5) significant developments in, or the resolution of, a matter
previously reported under these procedures.

b. Illegal activities include:

(1) An intelligence activity believed to be in violation of US
law, including any corrective action taken or planned in
connection with such activity;

(2) Significant misconduct by an employee of an IC element
or asset that is likely to seriously affect intelligence activities or
otherwise is of congressional concern, including human rights
violations; or

(3) Other serious violations of US criminal law by an
employee of an IC element or asset, which in the discretion of
the head of an IC element warrants congressional notification.

8. Criteria described in Sections D.6 and D.7 above are not
exhaustive. The absence of any of these criteria shall not be seen as
determinative. Each potential determination shall be addressed on its
particular merits. If it is unclear whether a notification is appropriate, IC
elements should decide in favor of notification. . . .

––––––––––––––

[NSL p. 579, CTL p. 192. Insert at the end of Note 6.]

The GPS issue was confronted by the Court in *United States v.
Jones*, 132 S. Ct. 945 (2012), where the Justices unanimously concluded
that Jones was searched when police attached a GPS device to the
undercarriage of his car and tracked his movements for four weeks. Yet
none of the three opinions expressly required that police obtain a warrant
for GPS tracking, and the opinions yielded no clear indication of the
nature or degree of suspicion that is required to attach a GPS device and
monitor the target's movements.

The opinion of the Court by Justice Scalia ruled that the
government's installation of the GPS device was a trespass, a physical
intrusion of private property that would have constituted a "search"
when the Fourth Amendment was ratified in 1791. Eschewing the *Katz*

"reasonable expectation of privacy" formula, Justice Scalia wrote that Fourth Amendment rights are based on the privacy that existed when the Fourth Amendment was adopted. According to Justice Scalia, to constitute a Fourth Amendment violation, in addition to the trespass, the government must have "attempt[ed] to find something or to obtain information." 132 S. Ct. at 951 n.5.

As the concurring Justices noted, the property-based approach of the majority did nothing to guide law enforcement or intelligence officials or the lower courts in determining the permissible uses of new surveillance technologies. Concurring in the judgment for himself and Justices Ginsburg, Breyer, and Kagan, Justice Alito would have applied *Katz* to decide *Jones*. *Id.* at 957-964. For Justice Alito, the long-term monitoring of Jones' movements, not the installation of the device on his car, violated his privacy. Justice Alito asked whether "GPS tracking in a particular case involve[s] a degree of instrusion that a reasonable person would not have anticipated." *Id.* at 964. Separately, Justice Sotomayor approved Justice Scalia's opinion, but also supported Justice Alito's *Katz*-based approach. She argued that the courts should take into account that "GPS monitoring generates a precise, comprehensive record of a person's public movements that reflects a wealth of detail about her familial, political, professional, religious, and sexual associations." *Id.* at 955.

Is an intrusiveness assessment any different from one based on a reasonable expectation of privacy? As Justice Alito noted, if an auto manufacturer installed a GPS in the cars it produces, the Court's theory would not protect the owner. What should be the Fourth Amendment rule for pre-installed GPS tracking? For the same tracking when GPS is pre-installed on cell phones? Or when some form of ID card, such as drivers' licenses or passports, is embedded with GPS capabilities, allowing the government to track every citizen's movements?

In *Knotts*, police discovered the location of a secluded drug lab by enclosing a beeper in a can of chloroform sold to one of the defendants. The can carrying the chloroform transmitted signals that enabled the police to track the defendant's car after earlier efforts to find the lab failed. *Knotts*, 460 U.S. at 278. Why isn't the GPS device used by the police in *Jones* simply an advanced beeper? The *Knotts* Court was careful to note that the beeper provided only location information, and that a car driving down the road is subject to scrutiny in that public space. The Court found no constitutional difference between traditional visual surveillance and this then-new form of electronic surveillance. *Id.* 460 U.S. at 281. Why should *Jones* be decided differently than *Knotts*?

[NSL p. 607, CTL p. 220. Insert at end of first paragraph of C. FISA Trends.]

Of 1,745 applications submitted to the FISC in calendar year 2011, 1,676 included requests for authority to perform electronic surveillance. The FISC did not deny any electronic surveillance applications in 2011, though it made modifications to 30 of them. *See* Letter from Ronald Welch, Assistant Attorney General, to Honorable Joseph R. Biden, Jr. (April 30, 2012), *available at* http://www.fas.org/irp/agency/doj/fisa/2011rept.pdf.

[NSL p. 629, CTL p. 242. Insert at the end of Note 3.]

At this writing, it appears that Congress is poised to extend the authorities in the FAA unchanged through June 2017. In June 2012, the Senate Intelligence Committee voted to recommend passage of S. 3276, the Foreign Intelligence Surveillance Act Amendments Act (FAA) Sunsets Extension Act, after defeating an amendment that would have explicitly prohibited searches of U.S. persons' communications that are inadvertently gathered in the course of authorized surveillance of foreign persons abroad, unless there was a warrant or other authorization permitting surveillance of the specific person. *FAA Sunsets Extension Act of 2012*, S. Rep. No. 112-174, 112th Cong. (June 7, 2012).

In their dissenting statement, Senators Ron Wyden and Mark Udall maintained that §1881a "contains a loophole that could be used to circumvent traditional warrant protections and search for the communications of a potentially large number of American citizens." *Id.* at 10. The Committee majority denied the existence of a loophole. Which side is correct? Can you identify the alleged loophole? If it exists, would the proposed amendment have closed it?

The Senate Intelligence Committee report conceded that incidental collection has occurred under the FAA, although the amount or frequency of such collection has not been quantified or specifically identified. *Id*. at 8-9. Are you persuaded that the statutory fix for over-collection — minimization — is adequate to protect the privacy interests of U.S. persons?

Three semi-annual reports on compliance with FAA procedures were released by the ODNI, in heavily redacted form. The reports found that "compliance incidents continue to occur," although investigators found no evidence of "any intentional or willful attempts to violate or circumvent the requirements of the Act." *Semiannual Assessment of Compliance with Procedures and Guidelines Issued Pursuant to Section 702 of the Foreign Intelligence Surveillance Act, Submitted by the Attorney General and the Director of National Intelligence*, reporting period: June 1, 2009-Nov. 30, 2009, May 2010, *available at* http://www.fas.org/irp/agency/doj/fisa/sar-may10.pdf.

[NSL p. 649, CTL p. 262. Insert after Note 5.]

6. *Requiem for Smith and Miller?* The assumptions underlying *Smith* and *Miller* may be eroding even in the Supreme Court. In a recent case in which the Court unanimously sustained a Fourth Amendment challenge to the use of a hidden GPS tracking device on a suspect's vehicle, Justice Sotomayor wrote in a concurring opinion:

> [I]t may be necessary to reconsider the premise that an individual has no reasonable expectation of privacy in information voluntarily disclosed to third parties. *E.g., Smith* [*v. Maryland*, 442 U.S. 735 (1979)], at 742; *United States v. Miller*, 425 U.S. 435 (1976). This approach is ill suited to the digital age, in which people reveal a great deal of information about themselves to third parties in the course of carrying out mundane tasks. People disclose the phone numbers that they dial or text to their cellular providers; the URLs that they visit and the e-mail addresses with which they correspond to their Internet service providers; and the books, groceries, and medications they purchase to online retailers. Perhaps, as Justice Alito notes, some people may find the "tradeoff" of privacy for convenience "worthwhile," or come to accept this "diminution of privacy" as "inevitable," *post*, at 962, and perhaps not. I for one doubt that people would accept without complaint the warrantless disclosure to the Government of a list of every Web site they had visited in the last week, or month, or year. But whatever the societal expectations, they can attain constitutionally protected status only if our Fourth Amendment jurisprudence ceases to treat secrecy as a prerequisite for privacy. I would

not assume that all information voluntarily disclosed to some member of the public for a limited purpose is, for that reason alone, disentitled to Fourth Amendment protection. See *Smith*, at 749 (Marshall, J., dissenting) ("Privacy is not a discrete commodity, possessed absolutely or not at all. Those who disclose certain facts to a bank or phone company for a limited business purpose need not assume that this information will be released to other persons for other purposes"); see also *Katz*, 389 U.S., at 351–352 ("[W]hat [a person] seeks to preserve as private, even in an area accessible to the public, may be constitutionally protected"). [*United States v. Jones*, 132 S. Ct. 945, 957 (2012).]

[NSL p. 677, CTL p. 290. Insert at end of chapter.]

Office of the Director of National Intelligence and Department of Justice Joint Statement: Revised Guidelines Issued to Allow the NCTC to Access and Analyze Certain Federal Data More Effectively to Combat Terrorist Threats

ODNI News Release No. 5-12, Mar. 22, 2012
available at
http://www.dni.gov/press_releases/20120322_Revised_Guidelines.pdf

Director of National Intelligence James R. Clapper, Attorney General Eric Holder, and National Counterterrorism Center (NCTC) Director Matthew G. Olsen have signed updated guidelines designed to allow NCTC to obtain and more effectively analyze certain data in the government's possession to better address terrorism-related threats, while at the same time protecting privacy and civil liberties.

The "Guidelines for Access, Retention, Use, and Dissemination by the National Counterterrorism Center (NCTC) of Information in Datasets Containing Non-Terrorism Information" effective Mar. 22, 2012, update November 2008 guidelines that governed NCTC s access, retention, use, and dissemination of "terrorism information" contained within federal datasets that are identified as also including non-terrorism information and information pertaining exclusively to domestic terrorism.

The updated Guidelines provide a framework that allows NCTC to obtain certain data held by other U.S. Government agencies to better protect the nation and its allies from terrorist attacks. In coordination with other federal agencies providing data to the NCTC, NCTC will establish the timeline for the retention of individual datasets based upon the type of data, the sensitivity of the data, any legal requirements that apply to the particular data, and other relevant considerations.

Among other modifications, the revised Guidelines:

- Permit NCTC to retain certain datasets that are likely to contain significant terrorism information and are already in the lawful custody and control of other federal agencies for up to five years, unless a shorter period is required by law.

- Permit NCTC to query this data only to identify information that is reasonably believed to constitute terrorism information.

- Provide that all data obtained by NCTC from another federal agency pursuant to the Guidelines, will be subject to appropriate safeguards and oversight mechanisms, including monitoring, recording, and auditing of access to and queries of the data, to protect privacy and civil liberties.

- Require NCTC to undertake a number of additional compliance and reporting obligations to ensure robust oversight.

The updated Guidelines do not provide any new authorities for the U.S. Government to collect information, nor do they authorize acquisition of data from entities outside the federal government. All information that would be accessed by NCTC under the Guidelines is already in the lawful custody and control of other federal agencies. The Guidelines merely provide the NCTC with a more effective means of accessing and analyzing datasets in the government's possession that are likely to contain significant terrorism information. They permit NCTC to consolidate disparate federal datasets that contain information of value to NCTC's critical counterterrorism mission. Furthermore, the updated Guidelines do not supersede or replace any legal restrictions on information sharing (existing by statute, Executive Order, regulation, or international agreement). Thus, the updated Guidelines do not give NCTC authority to require another agency to share any dataset where such sharing would contravene U.S. law or an international agreement.

One of the issues identified by Congress and the Intelligence

Community after the 2009 Fort Hood shootings and the Christmas Day 2009 bombing attempt was the government's limited ability to query multiple federal datasets and to correlate information from many sources that might relate to a potential attack. A review of government actions taken before these attacks recommended that the Intelligence Community push for the completion of state-of-the-art search and correlation capabilities, including techniques that would provide a single point of entry to various government databases.

"Following the failed terrorist attack in December 2009, representatives of the counterterrorism community concluded it is vital for NCTC to be provided with a variety of datasets from various agencies that contain terrorism information," said Clapper. "The ability to search against these datasets for up to five years on a continuing basis as these updated Guidelines permit will enable NCTC to accomplish its mission more practically and effectively than the 2008 Guidelines allowed." . . .

The 2008 Guidelines required NCTC to "promptly review" USP information and then "promptly remove" it if it is not reasonably believed to constitute terrorism information. This approach was a reasonable first step in 2008, but based on subsequent experience and lessons learned, the requirement to "promptly remove" USP information hampers NCTC's ability to identify terrorism information by connecting the dots across multiple datasets. . . .

Guidelines for Access, Retention, Use, and Dissemination by the National Counterterrorism Center and Other Agencies of Information in Datasets Containing Non-Terrorism Information

Mar. 22, 2012
available at http://www.fas.org/sgp/othergov/intel/nctc_guidelines.pdf

I. Background

A. Pursuant to section 119(d) of the National Security Act of 1947, as amended, the National Counterterrorism Center (NCTC) shall "serve as the primary organization in the United States Government for analyzing and integrating all intelligence possessed or acquired by the

United States Government pertaining to terrorism and counterterrorism, excepting intelligence pertaining exclusively to domestic terrorists and domestic counterterrorism." NCTC shall also "serve as the central and shared knowledge bank on known and suspected terrorists and international terror groups, as well as their goals, strategies, capabilities, and networks of contacts and support"; ensure that agencies "have access to and receive all-source intelligence support needed to execute their counterterrorism plans or perform independent, alternative analysis"; and "ensure that such agencies have access to and receive intelligence needed to accomplish their assigned activities." Furthermore, any agency "authorized to conduct counterterrorism activities may request information" from NCTC "to assist it in its responsibilities." *Id.* §119(e)(2). Finally, the Director of National Intelligence (DNI) also has significant responsibilities for information sharing. He has "principal authority to ensure maximum availability of and access to intelligence information" within the Intelligence Community (IC). *Id.* §102A(g)(1). When he establishes standards for facilitating access to and dissemination of information and intelligence, the DNI should give "the highest priority to detecting, preventing, preempting and disrupting terrorist threats and activities." Executive Order 12333 §1.3(b)(6)(A).

B. NCTC's analytic and integration efforts concerning terrorism and counterterrorism, as well as its role as the central and shared knowledge bank for known and suspected terrorists, at times require it to access and review datasets that are identified as including non-terrorism information in order to identity and obtain "terrorism information," as defined in section 1016 of the Intelligence Reform and Terrorism Prevention Act (IRTPA) of 2004, as amended.[1] "Non-terrorism information" for

---

1. "The term 'terrorism information' —

(A) means all information, whether collected. produced, or distributed by intelligence, law enforcement, military, homeland security, or other activities relating to —

(i) the existence, organization, capabilities, plans, intentions, vulnerabilities, means of finance or material support, or activities of foreign or international terrorist groups or individuals, or of domestic groups or individuals involved in transnational terrorism;

(ii) threats posed by such groups or individuals to the United States, United States persons, or United States interests, or to those of

purposes of these Guidelines includes information pertaining exclusively to domestic terrorism, as well as information maintained by other executive departments and agencies that has not been identified as "terrorism information" as defined by IRTPA. Included within those datasets identified as including non-terrorism information may be information concerning "United States persons," as defined in Executive Order 12333 of December 4, 1981, as amended. The President authorized the sharing of terrorism information in Executive Order 13388 of October 25, 2005, and required that agencies place the "highest priority" on the "interchange of terrorism information" in order to "strengthen the effective conduct of United States counterterrorism activities and protect the territory, people, and interests of the United States of America." That order further requires that the "head of each agency that possesses or acquires terrorism information . . . shall promptly give access to the terrorism information to the head of each other agency that has counterterrorism functions, and provide the terrorism information to each such agency," consistent with law and statutory responsibilities. In the National Security Act of 1947, as amended, Congress recognized that NCTC must have access to a broader range of information than it has primary authority to analyze and integrate it if is to achieve its missions. The Act thus provides that NCTC "may, consistent with applicable law, the direction of the President, and the guidelines referred to in section 102A(b), receive intelligence pertaining exclusively to domestic counterterrorism from any Federal, State, or local government or other source necessary to fulfill its responsibilities and retain and disseminate such intelligence." National Security Act of 1947, as amended, §119(e). Further, the Act envisions that NCTC, as part of the Office of the Director of National Intelligence (ODNI), *id.* §119(a), would have the broadest possible access to national intelligence relevant to terrorism and counterterrorism. Section 102A(b) of the National Security Act of 1947, as amended, provides that "[u]nless otherwise directed by the President, the Director of National Intelligence shall have access to all national intelligence and

---

other nations;
    (iii) communications for or by such groups or individuals; or
    (iv) groups or individuals reasonably believed to be assisting or associated with such groups or individuals; and
    (B) includes weapons of mass destruction information." 6 U.S.C. §485(a)(5).

intelligence related to the national security which is collected by any federal department, agency, or other entity, except as otherwise provided by law or, as appropriate, under guidelines agreed upon by the Attorney General and the Director of National Intelligence."

C. These Guidelines are established between the Attorney General and the Director of National Intelligence pursuant to section 102A(b) of the National Security Act of 1947, as amended, to govern the access, retention, use, and dissemination by NCTC of terrorism information that is contained within datasets maintained within other executive departments or agencies that are identified as including non-terrorism information. . . .

III. Guidelines

A. Authority for and Scope of NCTC Data Access and Acquisitions

1. *Purpose and Authority.* NCTC's access to, and acquisition, retention, use, and dissemination of, information covered by these Guidelines will be for authorized NCTC purposes. Pursuant to Executive Order 13388 and consistent with the National Security Act of 1947, as amended, and the March 4, 2003 Memorandum of Understanding between the Intelligence Community, Federal Law Enforcement Agencies, and the Department of Homeland Security Concerning Information Sharing, NCTC shall be afforded prompt access to all federal information and datasets that may constitute or contain terrorism information. NCTC may access or acquire datasets that may constitute or contain terrorism information, including those identified as containing non-terrorism information, such as information pertaining exclusively to domestic terrorism and other information maintained by executive departments and agencies that has not been identified as terrorism information, in order to acquire, retain, and disseminate terrorism information pursuant to NCTC's statutory authorities consistent with these Guidelines.

2. *United States Person Information.* These Guidelines permit NCTC to access and acquire United States person information for the purpose of determining whether the information is reasonably believed to constitute terrorism information and thus may be permanently

retained,[2] used, and disseminated. Any United States person information acquired must be reviewed for such purpose in accordance with the procedures below. Information is "reasonably believed to constitute terrorism information" if, based on the knowledge and experience of counterterrorism analysts as well as the factual and practical considerations of everyday life on which reasonable and prudent persons act, there are facts giving rise to a reasonable, articulable suspicion that the information is terrorism information.

3. *Erroneously Provided Information and Errors in Information.* Any United States person information that has been erroneously provided to NCTC will not be retained, used, or disseminated by NCTC. Such information will be promptly removed from NCTC's systems, unless such removal is otherwise prohibited by applicable law or court order or by regulation or policy approved by the Attorney General. Information in NCTC systems found to contain errors will be promptly corrected to ensure information integrity and accuracy, and the data provider shall be notified of the error when feasible.

4. *Applicable Laws and Policies.*

a) NCTC will access, acquire, retain, use, and disseminate information, including United States person information, (i) pursuant to the relevant standards of Executive Order 12333, as amended; (ii) as consistent with the National Security Act of 1947, as amended; and (iii) as authorized by law or regulations, including applicable privacy laws. These Guidelines do not apply to information the retention, use, and dissemination of which is governed by court order or court approved procedures.

b) NCTC shall not access, acquire, retain, use, or disseminate United States person information solely for the purpose of monitoring activities protected by the First Amendment or monitoring the lawful exercise of other rights secured by the Constitution or other laws of the United States. NCTC users of acquired information will be subject at all times to NCTC's Role-

---

2. For purposes of these Guidelines, "permanently retained" does not mean that the information is retained indefinitely, but rather that it is retained in accordance with NCTC's records retention policies.

Based Access and Information Sharing Policies, to applicable ODNI Instructions, and to additional audit and oversight authorities and requirements, as applicable. In implementing these Guidelines, NCTC shall consult with the ODNI General Counsel and the ODNI Civil Liberties Protection Officer, as appropriate.

5. *Responsibility for Compliance.* The Director of NCTC, in consultation with the ODNI Office of General Counsel, shall be the responsible official for ensuring that NCTC complies with these Guidelines. The ODNI Civil Liberties Protection Officer shall oversee compliance with these Guidelines and compliance with other applicable laws, regulations, guidelines, and instructions as they relate to civil liberties and privacy.

B. General Procedures for NCTC Data Access and Acquisitions

1. *Identification of Datasets.* NCTC will coordinate with the data provider to identify datasets that are reasonably believed to contain terrorism information, including those identified as containing non-terrorism information.

2. *Establishing Terms and Conditions for Information Access.*

a) For access to or acquisition of specific datasets, the DNI, or the DNI's designee, shall collaborate with the data provider to identify any legal constraints, operational considerations, privacy or civil rights or civil liberties concerns and protections, or other issues, and to develop appropriate Terms and Conditions that will govern NCTC's access to or acquisition of datasets under these Guidelines. If either party believes that the Terms and Conditions do not adequately address the matters identified during that collaboration, that party may raise those concerns in accordance with the procedures in section III.B.2(d), below. These Guidelines do not alter any other obligations of a data provider to provide information to the DNI or NCTC. All Terms and Conditions shall incorporate these Attorney General-approved Guidelines, and shall ensure that information is transmitted, stored, retained, accessed, used, and disseminated in a manner that (i) protects privacy and civil liberties and information integrity and security, and (ii) is in accordance with applicable laws, regulations, guidelines and instructions (including the ODNI's Privacy Instruction). NCTC and the data provider will establish procedures to ensure the data provider notifies NCTC of any information the data provider believes, or subsequently determines to be, materially inaccurate or unreliable. NCTC will ensure mechanisms are in place at NCTC to correct or document the inaccuracy or unreliability of such information, and supplement incomplete information to the extent additional information becomes available. NCTC will work with the data provider to ensure that data acquired by NCTC under these Guidelines is updated and verified throughout its retention and use by NCTC, in accordance with the data quality, data notice, redress, and other applicable provisions of the ODNI's Privacy Instruction. . . .

4. *Authorized Uses of Information.* Subject to any additional protections, requirements, or provisions in applicable Terms and Conditions, terrorism information, including terrorism information concerning United States persons, properly acquired and retained by NCTC may be used for all authorized NCTC purposes. These include, but are not limited to: analysis and integration purposes, inclusion in finished analytic products and pieces, enhancement of records contained within the Terrorist Identities Datamart Environment (TIDE), operational support, strategic operational planning, and appropriate dissemination to Intelligence Community elements, as well as federal and other counterterrorism partners. Specific provisions on use and dissemination are set forth in sections III.C and IV below, and any additional protections or provisions shall be specified in the Terms and Conditions. . . .

C. Specific Procedures for NCTC Data Access and Acquisitions

General. NCTC may acquire information contained within datasets governed by these Guidelines in one or more of the three ways outlined below. NCTC, in coordination with the data providers, will determine which information acquisition track, or tracks, provides the most effective means of ensuring NCTC access to terrorism information contained in the relevant datasets, consistent with the protection of privacy and civil liberties of United States persons, and any applicable legal requirements affecting provision of the specific data.

1. *Track I Information Acquisition: Account-Based Access*

a) *Type of Access.* NCTC personnel may be provided account-based access to the datasets of data providers that contain or may contain terrorism information (hereinafter "Track I" access).

b) *Standard.* NCTC will access information in such datasets identified as containing nonterrorism information only to determine if the dataset contains terrorism information. NCTC may acquire, retain, use, and disseminate terrorism information for all authorized NCTC purposes, as described in these Guidelines. If the information acquired by NCTC is subsequently determined not to constitute terrorism information, NCTC will promptly purge any information the retention, use, or dissemination of which is not authorized by sections IV [Dissemination] and V [Retention of Information for Administrative Purposes] below.

c) *Terrorism Datapoints.* Consistent with section 119 of the National Security Act of 1947, as amended, and section 1016(a)(5) of the IRTPA, as amended, the initial query term for NCTC Track 1 access shall be a known or suspected terrorist identifier or other piece of terrorism information (hereinafter "terrorism datapoints"). In order to follow up on positive query results, subsequent terrorism datapoints may be used to explore a known or suspected terrorist's network of contacts and support. NCTC's activities in Track 1 shall be designed to identify information that is reasonably believed to constitute terrorism information. NCTC is not otherwise permitted under these Guidelines to query, use, or exploit such datasets. For example, analysts may not browse through records in the dataset that do not match a query with terrorism datapoints, or conduct pattern-based queries or analyses without terrorism datapoints. . . .

2. *Track 2 Information Acquisition: Search and Retention*

a) *Type of Access.* NCTC may provide the owner of a dataset that contains or that may contain terrorism information with query terms — either singly or in batches — consisting of terrorism datapoints so that a search of the dataset may be run (hereinafter "Track 2" access).

b) *Standard.* Information from the dataset that is responsive to queries using NCTC-provided terrorism datapoints will be given by the data provider to NCTC. NCTC may acquire, retain, use, and disseminate information acquired under Track 2 for all authorized NCTC purposes, as described in these Guidelines. NCTC's activities in Track 2 shall be designed solely to identify information that is reasonably believed to be terrorism information. If the information given by a data provider to NCTC does not constitute terrorism information, NCTC will promptly purge any information whose retention, use, or dissemination is not authorized by sections IV and V below. . . .

3. *Track 3 Information Acquisition: NCTC Dataset Acquisition*

a) *Type of Access.* NCTC may acquire and replicate portions or the entirety of a dataset when necessary to identify the information that constitutes terrorism information within the dataset (hereinafter "Track 3" access).

b) *Standard and Process.* Replication of data is appropriate when the Director of NCTC, or a designee who serves as Principal Deputy Director or as a Deputy Director (hereinafter "Designee"), determines in writing, after coordination with the data provider, that a dataset is likely to contain significant terrorism information and that NCTC's authorized purposes cannot effectively be served through Tracks 1 or 2. When making a determination, the Director or Designee also shall consider whether NCTC's authorized purposes can effectively be served by the replication of a portion of a dataset. Datasets received in accordance with Track 3 may not be accessed or used by NCTC prior to replication, except as directly necessary to make the determination above or to accomplish such replication, subject to procedures agreed upon with the data provider. Measures will be put in place to ensure that the dataset is received and stored in a manner to prevent unauthorized access and use prior to the completion of replication.

c) *Identification of United States Person Information and Temporary Retention Period.* For all datasets received pursuant to Track 3, NCTC will use reasonable measures to identify and mark or tag United States person information contained within those datasets. Any United States person information acquired pursuant to Track 3 may be retained and continually assessed for a period of up to five years by NCTC to determine whether the United States person information is reasonably believed to constitute terrorism information (hereinafter "temporary retention period"). The Terms and Conditions shall establish the temporary retention period for continual assessment of such information. The temporary retention period specified in the Terms and Conditions may be up to five years unless a shorter period is required by law, including any statute, executive order, or regulation. In no event may NCTC retain the information for longer than is permitted by law. The temporary retention period shall commence when the data is made generally available for access and use following both the determination period discussed in section III.C.3(b) immediately above, and any necessary testing and formatting. United States person information that is reasonably believed to constitute terrorism information may be permanently retained and used for all authorized NCTC purposes, as described in these Guidelines.

   d) *Baseline Safeguards, Procedures, and Oversight Mechanisms.* During the temporary retention period, the following baseline safeguards, procedures, and oversight mechanisms shall apply to all datasets acquired pursuant to Track 3 that have been determined to contain United States person information:

   (1) These datasets will be maintained in a secure, restricted-access repository.

   (2) Access to these datasets will be limited to those NCTC personnel who are acting under, and agree to abide by, NCTC's information sharing and use rules, including these Guidelines; who have the requisite security clearance and a need-to-know in the course of their official duties; and who have received the training required by section 1II.B.3.

   (3) Access to these datasets will be monitored, recorded, and audited. This includes tracking of logons and logoffs, file and object manipulation and changes, and queries executed, in accordance with audit and monitoring standards applicable to the Intelligence Community. Audit records will be protected against unauthorized access, modifications, and deletion, and will be retained for a sufficient period to enable verification of compliance with rules applicable to the data for which audit records apply.

   (4) NCTC's queries or other activities to assess information contained in datasets acquired pursuant to Track 3 shall be designed solely to identify information that is reasonably believed to constitute terrorism information. NCTC shall query the data in a way designed to minimize the review of

information concerning United States persons that does not constitute terrorism information. To identify information reasonably believed to constitute terrorism information contained in Track 3 data, NCTC may conduct (i) queries that do not consist of, or do not consist exclusively of, terrorism data points, and (ii) pattern-based queries and analyses. To the extent that these activities constitute "data mining" as that term is defined in the Federal Agency Data Mining Reporting Act of 2007, the DNI shall report these activities as required by that Act. . . .

e) *Enhanced Safeguards, Procedures, and Oversight Mechanisms.* In addition to the requirements of paragraph (d), at the time when NCTC acquires a new dataset or a new portion of a dataset, the Director of NCTC or Designee shall determine, in writing, whether enhanced safeguards, procedures, and oversight mechanisms are needed. In making such a determination, the Director of NCTC or Designee shall (i) consult with the ODNI General Counsel and the ODNI Civil Liberties Protection Officer, and (ii) consider the sensitivity of the data; the purpose for which the data was originally collected by the data provider; the types of queries to be conducted; the means by which the information was acquired; any request or recommendation from the data provider for enhanced safeguards, procedures, or oversight mechanisms; the terms of any applicable international agreement regarding the data; the potential harm or embarrassment to a United States person that could result from improper use or disclosure of the information; practical and technical issues associated with implementing any enhanced safeguards, procedures, or oversight mechanisms; and all other relevant considerations. If the Director of NCTC or Designee determines that enhanced safeguards, procedures, and oversight mechanisms are appropriate, the determination shall include a description of the specific enhanced safeguards, procedures, or oversight mechanisms that will govern the continued retention and assessment of the dataset. These enhanced safeguards, procedures, or oversight mechanisms may include the following:

(1) Additional procedures for review, approval, and/or auditing of any access or searches;

(2) Additional procedures to restrict searches, access, or dissemination, such as procedures limiting the number of personnel with access or authority to search, establishing a

requirement for higher-level authorization or review before or after access or search, or requiring a legal review before or after United States person identities are unmasked or disseminated;

(3) Additional use of privacy enhancing technologies or techniques, such as techniques that allow United States person information or other sensitive information to be "discovered" without providing the content of the information, until the appropriate standard is met;

(4) Additional access controls, including data segregation, attribute-based access, or other physical or logical access controls;

(5) Additional, particularized training requirements for NCTC personnel given access or authority to search the dataset; and

(6) More frequent or thorough reviews of retention policies and practices to address the privacy and civil liberties concerns raised by continued retention of the dataset.

Any enhanced safeguards, procedures, and oversight mechanisms must be included in the Terms and Conditions, or specified in writing and appended to the Terms and Conditions, and shall be kept on file as required by NCTC's record retention schedule.

f) *Removal of Information.* NCTC shall remove from NCTC's systems all identified information concerning United States persons that NCTC does not reasonably believe constitutes terrorism information within five years from the date the data is generally available for assessment by NCTC (or within the time period identified in the Terms and Conditions if the Terms and Conditions specify a shorter temporary retention period), unless such removal is otherwise prohibited by applicable law or court order or by regulation or policy approved by the Attorney General, or unless the information is retained for administrative purposes as authorized in section V below. . . .

IV. Dissemination

A. General Dissemination Requirements

1. *Definition.* For purposes of these Guidelines, dissemination means transmitting, communicating, sharing, passing, or providing

access to information outside NCTC by any means, to include oral, electronic, or physical means.

2. *Terms and Conditions and Privacy Act.* All disseminations under these Guidelines must be: (i) compatible with any applicable Terms and Conditions or, if not compatible, the data provider must have otherwise consented to the dissemination; and (ii) permissible under the Privacy Act, 5 U.S.C. §552a, if applicable.

3. *Dissemination to State, Local, or Tribal Authorities or Private-Sector Entities.* These Guidelines are not intended to alter or otherwise impact pre-existing information sharing relationships by federal agencies with state, local, or tribal authorities or private-sector entities, whether such relationships arise by law, Presidential Directive, MOU, or other formal agreement (including, but not limited to, those listed in section II above). To the extent that these Guidelines allow for dissemination to state, local, tribal, or private sector entities, such dissemination will continue to be made, consistent with section 119(f)(1)(E) of the National Security Act (50 U.S.C. §404o(f)(1)(E)), in support of the Department of Justice (including the FBI) or the Department of Homeland Security responsibilities to disseminate terrorism information to these entities, and conducted under agreements with those Departments.

B. Dissemination of United States Person Information Acquired Under Tracks 1, 2, or 3

NCTC may disseminate United States person information properly acquired under Tracks 1, 2, or 3 if the General Dissemination Requirements are met, and if:

(1) *Dissemination of Terrorism Information.* The United States person information reasonably appears to constitute terrorism information, or reasonably appears to be necessary to understand or assess terrorism information, and NCTC is disseminating the information to a federal, state, local, tribal, or foreign or international entity, or to any other appropriate entity that is reasonably believed to have a need to receive such information for the performance of a lawful function;

(2) *Dissemination for Limited Purposes.* The United States person information is disseminated to other elements of the

Intelligence Community or to a federal, state, local, tribal, or foreign or international entity, or to any other appropriate entity, for the limited purpose of assisting NCTC in determining whether the United States person information constitutes terrorism information. Any such recipients may only use the information for this limited purpose, and may not use the information for any other purpose or disseminate the information further without the prior approval of NCTC. Recipients of information under this paragraph must promptly provide the requested assistance to NCTC and promptly thereafter return the information to NCTC or destroy it unless NCTC authorizes continued retention after the specific information is determined by NCTC to meet the dissemination criteria in section IV.C.1 of these Guidelines. Recipients of information under this paragraph may not retain the information for purposes of continual assessment of whether it constitutes terrorism information unless such retention would be permitted by the dissemination criteria in section IV.C.1. Any access to or dissemination under this paragraph of any bulk dataset or significant portion of a dataset believed to contain United States person information must be: (i) approved by the Director of NCTC; and (ii) expressly allowed by the Terms and Conditions or otherwise expressly approved by the data provider. In addition, the recipient of any bulk dataset or significant portion of a dataset under this provision must agree in writing that it: (i) will not disseminate the information further without prior approval by NCTC; (ii) will use the data solely for the limited purpose specified in this provision; (iii) will promptly return the data to NCTC or destroy it after providing the required assistance to NCTC, unless NCTC authorizes continued retention of specific information after it is determined by NCTC to meet the dissemination criteria in section IV.C.1 of these Guidelines; (iv) will comply with any safeguards and procedures deemed appropriate by the ODNI General Counsel and ODNI Civil Liberties Protection Officer; and (v) will report to NCTC any significant data breach or failure to comply with the terms of its agreement. In deciding whether to approve dissemination under this paragraph of any bulk dataset or significant portion of a dataset, the Director of NCTC shall consider whether the limited purpose of this paragraph can be satisfied by allowing access to the data while it remains under NCTC's control and whether the recipient of the data has the capabilities necessary to comply with the requirements specified above;

(3) *Dissemination Based on Consent.* The United States person whom the information concerns consents to the dissemination; or

(4) *Dissemination of Publicly Available Information.* The United States person information is publicly available.

C. Dissemination of United States Person Information Acquired Under Track 3

1. *Standard (Non-bulk) Dissemination of Specific Information Acquired Under Track 3.* In addition to the provisions above for dissemination under all three tracks, NCTC may disseminate specific United States person information acquired under Track 3 that has been handled and subsequently identified in accordance with applicable Track 3 safeguards and procedures, if the General Dissemination Requirements are met, and if the United States person information:

a) Reasonably appears to be foreign intelligence or counterintelligence, or information concerning foreign aspects of international narcotics activities, or reasonably appears to be necessary to understand or assess foreign intelligence, counterintelligence, or foreign aspects of international narcotics activities, and NCTC is disseminating the information to another federal, state, local, tribal, or foreign or international entity that is reasonably believed to have a need to receive such information for the performance of a lawful function, provided they agree to such further restrictions on dissemination as may be necessary;

b) Reasonably appears to be evidence of a crime, and NCTC is disseminating the information to another federal, state, local, tribal, or foreign agency that is reasonably believed to have jurisdiction or responsibility for the investigation or prosecution to which the information relates and a need to receive such information for the performance of a lawful governmental function;

c) Is disseminated to a Congressional Committee to perform its lawful oversight functions, after approval by the ODNI Office of General Counsel;

d) Is disseminated to a federal, state, local, tribal, or foreign or international entity, or to an individual or entity not part of a government, and is reasonably believed to be necessary to: (i) protect the safety or security of persons, property, or organizations; (ii) protect against or prevent a crime or a threat to the national security, provided they agree to such further restrictions on dissemination as may be necessary;

e) Is disseminated to another federal, state, local, tribal, or foreign or international entity for the purpose of determining the suitability or credibility of persons who are reasonably believed to be potential sources or contacts, provided they agree to such further restrictions on dissemination as may be necessary;

f) Is disseminated to another federal, state, local, tribal, or foreign or international entity for the purpose of protecting foreign intelligence or counterintelligence sources and methods from unauthorized disclosure;

g) Is disseminated to other recipients, if the subject of the information provides prior consent in writing;

h) Is otherwise required to be disseminated by statutes; treaties; executive orders; Presidential directives; National Security Council directives; Homeland Security Council directives; or Attorney General-approved policies, memoranda of understanding, or agreements; or

i) Is disseminated to appropriate elements of the Intelligence Community for the purposes of allowing the recipient element to determine whether the information is relevant to its responsibilities and can be retained by it.

The identity of a United States person may be disseminated outside the Intelligence Community only if it is necessary or if it is reasonably believed that it may become necessary to understand and assess such information.

2. *Bulk Dissemination of information Acquired Under Track 3 to IC Elements.* If the General Dissemination Requirements in section IV.A above are met, NCTC also may disseminate United States person information acquired under Track 3 to other IC elements under the following conditions . . . .

VI. Compliance

A. Periodic Compliance Reviews

Subject to oversight by the ODNI Civil Liberties Protection Officer, NCTC shall conduct periodic reviews to verify continued compliance with these Guidelines, including compliance with the Terms and Conditions, and with all baseline and enhanced safeguards, procedures, and oversight mechanisms. These reviews shall include spot checks, reviews of audit logs, and other appropriate measures. . . .

E. Privacy and Civil Liberties Oversight Board

Pursuant to section 1061 of the Intelligence Reform and Terrorism Prevention Act of 2004, the Privacy and Civil Liberties Oversight Board shall have access to all relevant NCTC records, reports, audits, reviews, documents, papers, recommendations, and other material that it deems relevant to its oversight of NCTC activities. . . .

VIII. Status as Internal Guidance

These Guidelines are set forth solely for the purpose of internal NCTC and ODNI guidance. They are not intended to, and do not, create any rights, substantive or procedural, enforceable at law or in equity, by any party against the United States, its departments, agencies, or entities, its officers, employees, agents, or any other person, nor do they place any limitation on otherwise lawful investigative or litigation prerogatives of the United States. . . .

NOTES AND QUESTIONS

1. *Not Connecting the Dots?* The solider charged with the Fort Hood shootings in 2009 (killing 13 and wounding 29) had been in email contact with Anwar al-Awlaki, a U.S.-born leader of Al Qaeda in the Arabian Peninsula who was later killed by the United States in a targeted killing in Yemen in 2011. Those communications were brought to the FBI's attention by a Joint Terrorism Task Force in 2008, but were missed because they seemed consistent with the soldier's supposed research on radical beliefs. After his arrest, the investigation revealed that the soldier had himself expressed radical beliefs in multiple contexts, but that no one in authority had connected the dots of his conduct with his emails. David Johnston & Scott Shane, *U.S. Knew of Suspect's Tie to Radical Cleric*, N.Y. Times, Nov. 9, 2009. The so-called "Christmas bomber" or "underwear bomber," whose attack on an airliner failed when a bomb he was carrying in his underwear misfired, had posted radical comments on the web before the attack and was also thought to have been in contact with al-Awlaki. British intelligence officers identified him by a pseudonym to U.S. authorities, and his own

father expressed concern about his radicalism to a U.S. Embassy before the attack, causing U.S. counterterrorism authorities to add his name to the Terrorist Identities Datamart Environment database. But it was not added to the Terror Screening Database, or, therefore, to the Secondary Screening Selectee list or No Fly List; nor was his U.S. visa revoked.

What dots were not connected in these cases, and why? Do the revised Guidelines close the gaps? Do they do much more? If so, can you guess why they were drafted the way they were?

2. *Terrorism and Non-Terrorism Information.* The press release suggests that the Guidelines make some minor modifications that will enable counterterrorism agencies to better connect dots of information about terrorism and to purge other information inadvertently collected along the way, subject to close privacy oversight. But precisely what information is it to which the Guidelines provide access? "Terrorism information" is defined in footnote 1, but §I.B explains that NCTC will also access datasets "that are identified as including non-terrorism information in order to identify and obtain 'terrorism information.'" OK, so what is "non-terrorism information"? This includes "information pertaining exclusively to domestic terrorism, as well as information maintained by other executive departments and agencies that has not been identified as 'terrorism information.'" §§I.B, III.A.1. May the NCTC thus gain access to all information that is terrorism information and all that isn't? What prevents these definitions from providing a perfect Orwellian moment[1] is that the non-terrorism information is apparently limited to that already maintained by other agencies.

Of course, given the power of government agencies to acquire information from regulated entities, to acquire it by National Security Letters, and to acquire it by other authorities, this may well be more than a few datasets. The Guidelines nowhere identify them, but one commentator speculates that "[t]hese datasets could contain information about credit card transactions, airline reservations, phone and ISP communications, bank, tax and social security records and perhaps even medical consultations." Christopher Slobogin, *The Future of Mass Dossiers*, Jurist-Forum, Apr. 11, 2012, *available at* http://jurist.org/forum/2012/04/christopher-slogobin-mass-dossiers.php.

---

1. *See* George Orwell, *1984.*

3. Retention and "Browsing" Restrictions. The Guidelines prohibit analysts from "brows[ing] through records in a [Track 1] dataset [account-based datasets of data providers] that do not match a query with terrorism datapoints, or conduct[ing] pattern-based queries or analyses without terrorism datapoints." §III(C)(1)(c). A "terrorism datapoint" is a "known or suspected terrorist identifier or other piece of terrorism information." *Id.* Alternatively, the NCTC can provide the owner of the dataset with query terms consisting of terrorism datapoints and the owner must then turn over responsive information to the NCTC (Track 2 information).

But the NCTC may also "acquire and replicate portions or the entirety of a dataset when necessary to identify the information that constitutes terrorism information within the dataset" (Track 3 access) if the director determines in writing that the dataset is "likely to contain significant terrorism information" and that NCTC's purposes cannot be served through Track 1 or 2. *Id.* §III(C)(3)(a)-(b). In Track 3 datasets, unlike Track 1 datasets,

> [t]o identify information reasonably believed to constitute terrorism information contained in Track 3 data, NCTC may conduct (i) queries that do not consist of, or do not consist exclusively of, terrorism data points, and (ii) pattern-based queries and analyses. [*Id.* §III(C)(3)(d)(4).]

In other words, NCTC is free to engage in broad datamining of Track 3 datasets without regard to terrorism datapoints. Moreover, the Guidelines expand the retention period for Track 3 datasets for U.S. persons from 180 days to five years.

Given the kinds of datasets to which the Guidelines can apply, can you envision what such datamining portends? Is it fair to speak of the possible creation of "mass dossiers" on U.S. persons? Slobogin, *supra* ("The know-it-all state is one that tends to be a state that oppresses, because those with knowledge are tempted to use it."). Was Justice Douglas ahead of his time or merely an alarmist when he said in dissent in a 1966 opinion:

> The dossiers on all citizens mount in number and increase in size. Now they are being put on computers so that by pressing one button all the miserable, the sick, the suspect, the unpopular, the offbeat people of the Nation can be instantly identified.
>
> These examples and many others demonstrate an alarming trend whereby the privacy and dignity of our citizens is being whittled away by

sometimes imperceptible steps. Taken individually, each step may be of little consequence. But when viewed as a whole, there begins to emerge a society quite unlike any we have seen — a society in which government may intrude into the secret regions of man's life at will. [*Osborn v. United States*, 385 U.S. 323, 342-343 (1966).]

4. *Protections.* Identify the protections set out in the Guidelines. Does a U.S. person whose information is "erroneously provided" to NCTC or who is erroneously identified as connected with terrorist information have any remedy?

[NSL p. 690, CTL p. 303. Insert after the *Gilmore* decision.]

Ibrahim v. Department of Homeland Security

United States Court of Appeals, Ninth Circuit, 2012
669 F.3d 983

W. FLETCHER, Circuit Judge: Plaintiff Rahinah Ibrahim is a citizen of Malaysia and mother of four children. She was legally in the United States from 2001 to 2005 as a Ph.D. student at Stanford University. She alleges that the U.S. government has mistakenly placed her on the "No-Fly List" and other terrorist watchlists. On January 2, 2005, she attempted to travel to a Stanford-sponsored conference in Malaysia where she was to present her doctoral research. She was prevented from flying and was detained in a holding cell for two hours at the San Francisco airport. She was allowed to fly to Malaysia the next day, but she was prevented from returning to the United States after the conference. Ibrahim has not been permitted to return to the United States.

Ibrahim brought suit in federal district court seeking, among other things, injunctive relief under the First and Fifth Amendments, with the ultimate aim of having her name removed from the government's watchlists. The district court denied injunctive relief. We reverse and remand for further proceedings.

I. Factual Background

A. Ibrahim's Departure . . .

[Ibrahim was stopped at the airport ticket counter when the airline employee discovered her name on the federal government's No-Fly List. After being detained by the police, she was permitted to go home and told that her name was no longer listed. But when she tried to fly out the next day, she was told that her name was back on the list. She was nonetheless permitted to fly out, but subsequently prevented from boarding a return flight. She filed a "Passenger Identity Verification" request with the TSA to clear her name, but it did not respond for a year.

In the meantime, the Department of State revoked her student visa citing] Ibrahim's "possible ineligibility" under §212(a)(3)(B) of the Immigration & Nationality Act (INA) as the reason for the revocation. That section of the INA provides, among other things, that "[a]ny alien" (1) who "has engaged in terrorist activity"; (2) who "a consular officer, the Attorney General, or the Secretary of Homeland Security knows, or has reasonable ground to believe, is engaged in or is likely to engage after entry in any terrorist activity"; or (3) who "has, under circumstances indicating an intention to cause death or serious bodily harm, incited terrorist activity," is inadmissible to the United States. 8 U.S.C. §1182(a)(3)(B). . . .

B. The Government's Terrorist Watchlists

Since the terrorist attacks of September 11, 2001, the federal government has assembled a vast, multi-agency, counterterrorism bureaucracy that tracks hundreds of thousands of individuals. *See, e.g.,* 6 U.S.C. §§122, 124h, 482, 485; Exec. Order No. 13388, 70 Fed. Reg. 62023 (Oct. 25, 2005). At the heart of this bureaucracy is the Terrorist Screening Center ("TSC"). Established by the Attorney General in 2003 pursuant to a presidential directive, the mission of TSC is "to consolidate the Government's approach to terrorism screening and provide for the appropriate and lawful use of Terrorist Information in screening processes." *See* Homeland Security Presidential Directive/ HSPD-6. Though administered by the FBI, TSC retains personnel from the Departments of State, Homeland Security, and Defense, and other federal agencies.

TSC manages the Terrorist Screening Database ("TSDB"), the federal government's centralized watchlist of known and suspected terrorists. The National Counterterrorism Center nominates known and suspected international terrorists to the TSDB, while the FBI nominates known and suspected domestic terrorists. TSC distributes subsets of the TSDB to other federal agencies to help implement the government's counterterrorism initiatives. TSA uses two subsets of the TSDB — the No-Fly List and the Selectee List — to screen airline passengers. Individuals on the No-Fly List are prohibited from boarding American carriers or any flight having virtually any contact with U.S. territory or airspace. Individuals on the Selectee List are subject to enhanced security screening before boarding an airplane. The State Department uses a subset of the TSDB to screen visa applicants through the Consular Lookout and Support System.

The evidence and procedures used to nominate individuals to the TSDB are kept secret from the general public, as are the names of those in the TSDB. However, thousands of front line law enforcement officers from federal, state, local, territorial, and tribal agencies have access to the TSDB, as do some private sector entities and individuals. As of January 2011, TSC had also agreed to share information with 22 foreign governments.

Since its inception, the TSDB has grown by more than 700%, from about 158,000 records in June 2004 to over 1.1 million records in May 2009. In 2007, these records contained information on approximately 400,000 individuals. As of 2007, the TSDB was increasing at a rate of 20,000 records per month. TSC makes 400 to 1200 changes to the TSDB every day. It is the "world's most comprehensive and widely shared database of terrorist identities."

In theory, only individuals who pose a threat to civil aviation are put on the No-Fly and Selectee Lists, but the Justice Department has criticized TSC for its "weak quality assurance process." In July 2006 — after the events that gave rise to this lawsuit — there were 71,872 records in the No-Fly List. After an internal review, TSC downgraded 22,412 records from the No-Fly List to the Selectee List and deleted entirely an additional 5,086 records. By January 2007, the TSC had cut the No-Fly List by more than half, to 34,230 records. Tens of thousands of travelers have been misidentified because of misspellings and transcription errors in the nomination process, and because of computer algorithms that imperfectly match travelers against the names on the list. TSA maintains a list of approximately 30,000 individuals who are commonly confused with those on the No-Fly and Selectee Lists. One major air carrier reported that it encountered 9,000 erroneous terrorist watchlist matches every day during April 2008.

Nomination and identification errors are so common that TSC organized a redress unit in 2007 to deal with complaints. The redress procedures have been opaque. A 2006 GAO report stated that an individual who submitted a query to TSC's redress unit received an initial response letter that "neither confirms nor denies the existence of any terrorist watch list records relating to the individual." A 2009 internal DHS report stated, "With few exceptions, redress-seekers receive response letters that do not reveal the basis for their travel difficulties, the action the government took to address those difficulties, or other steps that they may take to help themselves in the future."

When Ibrahim filed suit, TSA managed a Passenger Identity Verification program for travelers who believed that they were mistakenly put on the No-Fly or Selectee List. In place of that program, the Department of Homeland Security ("DHS") now manages the Traveler Redress Inquiry Program ("TRIP"). A 2007 Department of Justice audit commended TSC for accurately resolving redress queries, but noted that 45% of the reviewed records contained an error. The 2009 DHS report was less charitable, concluding that the "TRIP website advises travelers that the program can assist them with resolving a range of travel difficulties. Our review of redress results revealed that those claims are overstated. While TRIP offers effective solutions to some traveler issues, it does not address other difficulties effectively, including the most common — watch list misidentifications in aviation security settings."

II. Procedural Background

[Irahim filed suit against DHS, TSA, TSC, the FBI, the Federal Aviation Administration ("FAA"), and individuals associated with these entities (collectively, "the federal defendants"), as well as various state and local entities, asserting a variety of constitutional and state law tort claims. She sought an injunction that would require the government to take her name off its terrorist watch lists, including the No-Fly List, or, in the alternative, to provide procedures under which she could challenge her inclusion on those lists. After proceedings not here relevant, the district court dismissed her claims, accepting the government argument that Ibrahim has no right to assert claims under the

First and Fifth Amendments because she is an alien who has voluntarily left the United States. She appealed that dismissal and other rulings omitted here.] . . .

IV. Discussion . . .

B. Constitutional Claims

Claim 13 . . . alleges that the placement of Ibrahim's name on the government's terrorist watchlists violates her right to freedom of association under the First Amendment and her rights to equal protection and due process under the Fifth Amendment.

At this point in the litigation, no court has attempted to determine the merits of Ibrahim's claims under the First and Fifth Amendments. The parties have not briefed whether her placement on a terrorist watchlist violates her rights to freedom of association, equal protection, and due process. The only question before us is whether Ibrahim even has the right to assert such claims.

We begin with the uncontested proposition that if Ibrahim had remained in the United States, she would have been able to assert claims under the First and Fifth Amendments to challenge her placement on the government's terrorist watchlists. It is well established that aliens legally within the United States may challenge the constitutionality of federal and state actions. Even aliens who are in the United States illegally may bring constitutional challenges, *see, e.g., Plyler v. Doe,* 457 U.S. 202, 211–12 (1982); *Wong Wing v. United States,* 163 U.S. 228, 237 (1896), including the ability to challenge the revocation of a visa. The question in this case is whether Ibrahim lost the right she otherwise had because she left the United States.

The Supreme Court has held in a series of cases that the border of the United States is not a clear line that separates aliens who may bring constitutional challenges from those who may not. For example, a resident alien who voluntarily leaves the United States on a brief trip with an intent to return is constitutionally entitled to a due process hearing if the government seeks to exclude her upon return to the United States. *See, e.g., Landon v. Plasencia,* 459 U.S. 21, 34 (1982) (resident alien entitled to constitutional due process hearing in exclusion proceedings upon re-entry after a "few days" abroad); *Rosenberg v. Fleuti,* 374 U.S. 449, 450 (1963) (entry after innocent, casual, and brief excursion abroad did not qualify as "entry" for immigration purposes);

Kwong Hai Chew, 344 U.S. at 593–95 (resident alien entitled to constitutional due process hearing after exclusion following a five-month voyage abroad). *See also Boumediene v. Bush,* 553 U.S. 723 (2008) (aliens held as enemy combatants outside the *de jure* sovereign territory of the United States may petition for habeas corpus to challenge the constitutionality of their detention); *Al Maqaleh v. Gates,* 605 F.3d 84, 95–96 (D.C. Cir. 2010) (location of alien outside the United States is only a factor in determining the extraterritorial reach of the Constitution); *Nat'l Council of Resistance of Iran v. Dep't of State,* 251 F.3d 192 (D.C. Cir. 2001) (a foreign organization with property in the United States entitled to constitutional due process hearing before Secretary of State may classify it as a "foreign terrorist organization"); *Cardenas v. Smith,* 733 F.2d 909, 915 (D.C. Cir. 1984) (Colombian national outside the United States entitled to assert due process claim against U.S. government based on seizure of her Swiss bank account); *In re Aircrash in Bali, Indonesia on April 22, 1974,* 684 F.2d 1301, 1308 n.6 (9th Cir. 1982) (nonresident aliens suing on same cause of action as citizens have the right to assert takings claim).

In *United States v. Verdugo-Urquidez,* 494 U.S. 259 (1990), the Supreme Court wrote that "aliens receive constitutional protections when they have come within the territory of the United States and developed substantial connections with this country." *Id.* at 271. The Court's statement in *Verdugo-Urquidez* was an elaboration of its earlier language in *Johnson v. Eisentrager,* 339 U.S. 763 (1950), that an alien "is accorded a generous and ascending scale of rights as he increases his identity with our society." *Verdugo-Urquidez,* 494 U.S. at 269 (quoting *Eisentrager,* 339 U.S. at 770) (internal quotations omitted). The Court wrote in *Boumediene* that the right of an alien outside the United States to assert constitutional claims is based on "objective factors and practical concerns" rather than "formalism." 553 U.S. at 764. In determining the constitutional rights of aliens outside the United States, the Court applies a "functional approach" rather than a bright-line rule. *Id.*

A comparison of Ibrahim's case with *Verdugo-Urquidez, Eisentrager,* and *Boumediene* is instructive.

In *Verdugo-Urquidez,* plaintiff had been arrested in Mexico and brought against his will to the Mexico-United States border, where he was turned over to United States authorities and imprisoned in the United States while awaiting trial on narcotics smuggling charges. The Court held that the plaintiff had "no previous *significant voluntary connection* with the United States" and therefore had no right to assert a Fourth Amendment challenge to searches and seizures of his property by United States agents in Mexico. *Verdugo-Urquidez,* 494 U.S. at 271 (emphasis added).

Relying on *Verdugo-Urquidez,* the government insists that Ibrahim left the United States "voluntarily" and that she thereby forfeited any right to assert constitutional claims she might have had if she had remained in the United States. The government mistakes the nature of the *Verdugo-Urquidez* inquiry. Under *Verdugo-Urquidez,* the inquiry is whether the alien has voluntarily established a connection with the United States, not whether the alien has voluntarily left the United States. The circumstances of an alien's departure may cast some light on whether the alien has established, and wishes to maintain, a voluntarily established connection with the United States. But the mere fact that an alien's departure is voluntary tells us very little. In Ibrahim's case, she left the United States to attend a Stanford-sponsored conference to present her academic research, performed in connection with her Ph.D. studies at Stanford, and she expected to return to Stanford after the conference to complete her studies. Ibrahim thus did not intend to sever her established connection to the United States by her voluntary departure, but rather to develop that connection further.

In *Eisentrager,* the plaintiffs were German citizens who had been arrested in China, convicted of violating the laws of war after adversary trials before a U.S. military tribunal in China, and sent to a prison in Germany to serve their sentences. The Supreme Court held that they did not have a right to seek a writ of habeas corpus under our Constitution. The Court summarized:

> [To agree with plaintiffs that they are entitled to seek habeas] we must hold that a prisoner of our military authorities is constitutionally entitled to the writ, even though he (a) is an enemy alien; (b) has never been or resided in the United States; (c) was captured outside of our territory and there held in military custody as a prisoner of war; (d) was tried and convicted by a Military Commission sitting outside the United States; (e) for offenses against laws of war committed outside the United States; (f) and is at all times imprisoned outside the United States.

339 U.S. at 777.

Ibrahim's case is unlike that of the plaintiffs in *Eisentrager.* She has not been convicted of, or even charged with, any violation of law. She is a citizen of a country with which we have never been at war. She contends that the placement of her name on the government's terrorist watchlists is a mistake. Her contention is not implausible, given the frequent mistakes the government has made in placing names on these lists. She has established a substantial voluntary connection with the United States through her Ph.D. studies at a distinguished American university, and she wishes to maintain that connection.

In *Boumediene,* the plaintiffs were aliens who had been designated as enemy combatants and who were detained at the United States Naval Station in Guantanamo. Plaintiffs had not been tried or convicted of any crime. They sought federal habeas corpus. The government argued that because plaintiffs were aliens who had committed acts outside the United States and were being detained outside the United States, they were not entitled to seek habeas relief. The Court rejected the government's proposed bright-line rule, calling it a "formal, sovereignty-based test." 553 U.S. at 764. The Court wrote that while the United States does not have *de jure* sovereignty over the Naval Station at Guantanamo Bay, it "maintains *de facto* sovereignty." *Id.* at 755. Applying a "functional approach," *id.* at 764, the Court held that the plaintiffs in *Boumediene,* unlike the plaintiffs in *Eisentrager*, had a right to seek a writ of habeas corpus.

Ibrahim shares an important similarity with the plaintiffs in *Boumediene.* The *Boumediene* plaintiffs and Ibrahim both sought (or seek) the right to assert constitutional claims in a civilian court in order to correct what they contend are mistakes. In *Boumediene,* plaintiffs sought the right to try to establish they were not, in fact, enemy combatants. Ibrahim seeks the right to try to establish that she does not, in fact, deserve to be placed on the government's watchlists.

The government in *Boumediene* proposed a bright-line "formal sovereignty-based test" under which the absence of *de jure* jurisdiction over Guantanamo would have meant that plaintiffs had no right to seek habeas corpus under the Constitution. The Court disagreed, adopting instead a "functional approach" under which the absence of *de jure* jurisdiction was not determinative. *Id.* at 764. The government proposes a similar bright-line "formal sovereignty-based test" in Ibrahim's case. Under the government's proposed test in this case, any alien, no matter how great her voluntary connection with the United States, immediately loses all constitutional rights as soon as she voluntarily leaves the country, regardless of the purpose of her trip, and regardless of the length of her intended stay abroad. The government's proposed test is not the law. The law that we are bound to follow is, instead, the "functional approach" of *Boumediene* and the "significant voluntary connection" test of *Verdugo-Urquidez.*

Under *Boumediene* and *Verdugo-Urquidez,* we hold that Ibrahim has "significant voluntary connection" with the United States. She voluntarily established a connection to the United States during her four years at Stanford University while she pursued her Ph.D. She voluntarily departed from the United States to present the results of her research at a Stanford-sponsored conference. The purpose of her trip was to further, not to sever, her connection to the United States, and she intended her stay abroad to be brief.

We do not hold that tourists, business visitors, and all student visa holders have the same connection to the United States as Ibrahim. Nor do we hold that Congress is without authority to exclude undesirable aliens from the United States and to prescribe terms and conditions for entry and re-entry of aliens. We hold only that Ibrahim has established "significant voluntary connection" with the United States such that she has the right to assert claims under the First and Fifth Amendments. Like the Court in *Boumediene,* we express no opinion on the validity of the underlying constitutional claims. . . .

Conclusion

We hold that Ibrahim has significant voluntary connection to the United States and she may therefore assert claims against the federal defendants for prospective relief under the First and Fifth Amendments. . . .

We REVERSE in part, [and for reasons not relevant here] AFFIRM in part, and VACATE in part. We REMAND for further proceedings consistent with this opinion. Costs to Appellant.

DUFFY, District Judge: I dissent. . . .

The majority relies on a number of cases to show that certain aliens located outside the United States can challenge the constitutionality of U.S. laws. One such case is *Kwong Hai Chew v. Colding,* 344 U.S. 590 (1953). . . . [But in *Kwong,*][t]he Supreme Court recognized that, while Kwong Hai Chew was on the high seas, he was at all times under the jurisdiction of the United States, as evidenced by the American flag on the S.S. Sir John Franklin.

. . . In the instant case, Petitioner resides in Malaysia and, therefore, does not enjoy the right of constitutional challenge.

Slightly more instructive on the issue of whether aliens located outside of the United States can bring constitutional claims is *Boumediene v. Bush,* 553 U.S. 723 (2008). . . . [In that case,] [t]he Supreme Court's decision did not disregard the extraterritoriality of the claims being asserted, but focused instead on the fact that Boumediene and his fellow petitioners held at Guantánamo Bay were in U.S. custody following capture in, and transfer from, various foreign lands. Here, the Petitioner, knowing that she could be forever banned from returning to this country, voluntarily left and returned to her native land, outside of U.S. jurisdiction. No one can believe that she did not know exactly the consequences of the choice she made.

In *Johnson v. Eisentrager,* 339 U.S. 763 (1950), a group of German nationals sought the writ of habeas corpus after being arrested by the United States Army in China, convicted of violating the laws of war by a Military Commission sitting in China, and imprisoned in Germany. . . . [L]ike the petitioners in *Eisentrager,* the Petitioner does not find herself under U.S. jurisdiction, whether *de jure* or *de facto,* as did the petitioners in *Boumediene.*

I must also note a crucial distinction between *Boumediene* and *Eisentrager* on the one hand and the present case on the other. The petitioners in the habeas cases cited above sought to challenge their detention at U.S. hands, whereas the Petitioner is not in our custody and therefore can have no grounds on which to seek similar relief. . . .

The majority distinguishes *Verdugo-Urquidez* by finding that Petitioner "established a substantial voluntary connection with the United States through her studies at a distinguished American university." I cannot come to the same conclusion. If we were to hold today that Petitioner may assert her constitutional claims because she formed a "substantial voluntary connection with the United States" while here on a student visa, then we would be hard pressed not to allow all alien students who studied in the United States and subsequently left the country to bring constitutional claims in our courts.

. . . If this were sufficient to vest constitutional rights in an alien located outside of the United States to bring actions in the United States against the government, there would be a significant number of aliens in the world just waiting to get into court. For example, a visitor to this country who overstays his visa, makes a livelihood in this country for a substantial amount of time, and chooses voluntary departure when caught as an illegal alien, could fit within the class of people who would have such rights. He would have been in the country for a "substantial time" and would have friends and contacts in this country — as would most illegal aliens. As such, he would most likely have the desire and intention to return to this country.

As this example shows, the majority holding is too broad, while the government's bright line argument based on extraterritoriality is too narrow and hidebound for use in the modern world.

In the case at bar, however, there is no need to set forth a definitive test because the simple answer is that Petitioner has not shown a "substantial voluntary connection" with the United States, which is the measurement the majority believes the precedent would require. The Petitioner does not suggest that she ever worked in or paid taxes to the United States or indeed did anything (except study at a university) to indicate that she ever made a conscious decision to live in this country or to accept any of the responsibilities of a permanent resident. She merely came to acquire the education available and thereby improve her position in her own native country. Obviously, the Petitioner is quite content in having advanced from assistant professor at the University Putra Malaysia prior to obtaining her doctorate to associate professor and Deputy Dean of that university now. At all times that she was in the United States, her main objective was to personally benefit from this country. Any contribution the Petitioner made to the United States was incidental to this objective. That, to my mind, is totally insufficient to constitute a substantial voluntary connection. . . .

[NSL p. 810, CTL p. 424. Insert after the *Rasul* decision.]

Al-Zahrani v. Rodriguez

United States Court of Appeals, District of Columbia Circuit, 2012
669 F.3d 315

[Relatives of two non-citizens who died while detained as "enemy combatants" at Guantánamo Bay brought suit seeking damages arising from the alleged mistreatment and eventual death of the detainees. In its earlier decision in *Rasul v. Myers*, 563 F.3d 527 (D.C. Cir. 2009) (per curiam) (*Rasul II*), the Court of Appeals held that Guantánamo detainees could not pursue damages claims for constitutional violations against federal officials because (1) no clearly established law existed with respect to the detainees' constitutional rights (and so the defendants were entitled to qualified immunity), and, in any event, (2) "special factors" counseled hesitation with respect to recognizing a *Bivens* remedy for Guantánamo detainees. In another earlier decision, *Ali v. Rumsfeld*, 649 F.3d 762 (D.C. Cir. 2011), the Court of Appeals likewise concluded that Guantánamo detainees could not pursue claims under the Alien Tort Statute, 28 U.S.C. §1350. The district court relied on these decisions in dismissing the plaintiffs' claims. In the following opinion, the Court of Appeals affirmed, albeit for different — and broader — reasons.]

SENTELLE, Chief Judge: . . .

Background

. . . Beginning in January of 2002, Yasser Al-Zahrani, Jr., a citizen of Saudi Arabia, and Salah Ali Abdullah Ahmed Al-Salami, Jr., a citizen of Yemen, were detained at the United States military base at Guantanamo Bay, Cuba, as "enemy combatants." In 2004, under the then-current procedure of the United States military, [CSRTs] reviewed the detention of the two and confirmed the earlier determination that both detainees were enemy combatants. On June 10 of 2006, both men, along with a third detainee, died. Although the cause of death is the subject of dispute in the current litigation, a Naval Criminal Investigative Service report concluded that the deaths were the result of suicide by hanging.

On January 7, 2009, the plaintiffs, as fathers of the two named decedents, filed an action against the United States, twenty-four named, current, or former officials of the United States, and one hundred unnamed "John Doe" officials of the United States, seeking money damages relating to the deaths of the two detainees and alleging that the defendants had subjected the decedents to torture, arbitrary detention, and ultimately, wrongful death. The defendants moved for the dismissal of plaintiffs' by-then amended complaint. The district court dismissed the complaint pursuant to Rule 12(b)(6) of the Federal Rules of Civil Procedure for failure to state a claim upon which relief could be granted.

For the reasons more fully set forth below, we affirm the judgment of dismissal, although we further hold that the dismissal is for a lack of jurisdiction rather than the failure to state a claim for relief.

Analysis

. . . Because a federal court without jurisdiction cannot perform a law-declaring function in a controversy, "the Supreme Court [has] held 'that Article III jurisdiction is always an antecedent question' to be answered prior to any merits inquiry." *Public Citizen v. U.S. District Court for the District of Columbia*, 486 F.3d 1342, 1346 (D.C. Cir. 2007) (quoting *Steel Co. v. Citizens for a Better Env't*, 523 U.S. 83, 101 (1998)). Therefore, rather than proceed to weigh the adequacy of the complaint to state a claim, as did the District Court, we first examine the jurisdiction of the courts to entertain plaintiffs' claims and find that jurisdiction wanting.

In October of 2006, Congress enacted the Military Commissions Act. Section 7 of the MCA included an amendment to the habeas corpus statute. The amended statute reads:

> (1) No court, justice, or judge shall have jurisdiction to hear or consider an application for a writ of habeas corpus filed by or on behalf of an alien detained by the United States who has been determined by the United States to have been properly detained as an enemy combatant or is awaiting such determination.
>
> (2) Except as provided in [section 1005(e)(2) and (e)(3) of the Detainee Treatment Act of 2005], no court, justice, or judge shall have jurisdiction to hear or consider any other action against the United States or its agents relating to any aspect of the detention, transfer, treatment, trial, or conditions of confinement of an alien who is or was detained by the United States and has been determined by the United States to have been properly detained as an enemy combatant or is awaiting such determination.

28 U.S.C. §2241(e)(1) and (2).

The present litigation rather plainly constitutes an action other than habeas corpus brought against the United States and its agents relating to "aspect[s] of the detention . . . treatment . . . [and] conditions of confinement of an alien" as described in the MCA. Therefore, as the District Court noted, this action is excluded from the jurisdiction of this court by the "plain language" of an Act of Congress. This ends the litigation and requires that we affirm the dismissal of the action.

. . . It is true that the Supreme Court, in its review of our decision in *Boumediene*, found §7 of the MCA to be constitutionally defective. *Boumediene v. Bush*, 553 U.S. 723, 787-92 (2008). However, the *Boumediene* appeal involved a decision applying the first subsection of

§7 governing and barring the hearing of applications for writs of habeas corpus filed by detained aliens. . . . Subsection 2 of the MCA, which governs and bars the present litigation, has no effect on habeas jurisdiction. The Suspension Clause is not relevant and does not affect the constitutionality of the statute as applied in "treatment" cases [such as this one]. . . .

Appellants argue that §2241(e)(2)'s jurisdictional bar is unconstitutional because it fails to provide a proper remedy for violations of their constitutional rights. But the only remedy they seek is money damages, and, as the government rightly argues, such remedies are not constitutionally required. The Supreme Court has made this eminently clear in its jurisprudence finding certain of such claims barred by common law or statutory immunities, and applying its "special factors" analysis in preclusion of *Bivens* claims. Further, the Court applies that analysis to preclude *Bivens* claims even in cases such as the present one, where damages are the sole remedy by which the rights of plaintiffs and their decedents might be vindicated. For example, in *United States v. Stanley*, the Court refused to create a *Bivens* cause of action for a military serviceman who had been secretly administered doses of LSD; in doing so, the Court noted that it was "irrelevant to [the analysis] whether the laws currently on the books afford Stanley . . . an 'adequate' federal remedy for his injuries." 483 U.S. 669, 683 (1987). As we have recently said, "Not every violation of a right yields a remedy, even when the right is constitutional." *Kiyemba v. Obama*, 555 F.3d 1022, 1027 (D.C. Cir. 2009), *reinstated as amended by Kiyemba v. Obama*, 605 F.3d 1046 (D.C. Cir. 2010) [(per curiam)]. In light of this, we see no basis on which to invalidate Congress's decision to foreclose such claims as plaintiffs'.

Conclusion

. . . [W]e hold that 28 U.S.C. §2241(e)(2) deprives this court of jurisdiction over appellants' claims. We further hold that the Supreme Court did not declare §2241(e)(2) unconstitutional in *Boumediene* and the provision retains vitality to bar those claims. We therefore conclude that the decision of the District Court dismissing the claims should be affirmed, although for a lack of jurisdiction under Rule 12(b)(1) rather than for failure to state a claim under Rule 12(b)(6).

[NSL p. 810, CTL p. 424. Insert after Note 2.]

3. *Jurisdiction-Stripping and Bivens Claims. Al-Zahrani* holds that Congress validly took away federal jurisdiction over *Bivens* suits for damages by former Guantánamo detainees because, unlike the habeas remedy at issue in *Boumediene v. Bush*, 553 U.S. 723 (2008), "such remedies are not constitutionally required." Although the Supreme Court has never identified a case in which the Constitution *does* require a damages remedy for a violation of a specific constitutional provision, it has never expressly forsworn such a possibility, either. Indeed, it has repeatedly alluded to the "'serious constitutional question' that would arise if a federal statute were construed to deny any judicial forum for a colorable constitutional claim," *Webster v. Doe*, 486 U.S. 592, 603 (1988), as the D.C. Circuit construes the MCA in *Al-Zahrani*. Given that, should the D.C. Circuit have done more to explain why the MCA validly divested the courts of jurisdiction? More fundamentally, why didn't *Al-Zahrani* simply rely on *Rasul*?

[NSL p. 852, CTL p. 466. Insert after Note 2.]

Jeh Charles Johnson, General Counsel of the Department of Defense, National Security Law, Lawyers and Lawyering in the Obama Administration

Remarks at Yale Law School, Feb. 22, 2012
available at http://www.lawfareblog.com/2012/02/jeh-johnson-speech-at-yale-law-school/

. . .

. . . [T]he AUMF, the statutory authorization from 2001, is not open-ended. It does not authorize military force against anyone the Executive labels a "terrorist." Rather, it encompasses only those groups or people with a link to the terrorist attacks on 9/11, or associated forces.

Nor is the concept of an "associated force" an open-ended one, as some suggest. This concept, too, has been upheld by the courts in the detention context, and it is based on the well-established concept of co-belligerency in the law of war. The concept has become more relevant over time, as al Qaeda has, over the last 10 years, become more de-centralized, and relies more on associates to carry out its terrorist aims.

An "associated force," as we interpret the phrase, has two characteristics to it: (1) an organized, armed group that has entered the fight alongside al Qaeda, and (2) is a co-belligerent with al Qaeda in hostilities against the United States or its coalition partners. In other words, the group must not only be aligned with al Qaeda. It must have also entered the fight against the United States or its coalition partners. Thus, an "associated force" is not any terrorist group in the world that merely embraces the al Qaeda ideology. More is required before we draw the legal conclusion that the group fits within the statutory authorization for the use of military force passed by the Congress in 2001.

Third: there is nothing in the wording of the 2001 AUMF or its legislative history that restricts this statutory authority to the "hot" battlefields of Afghanistan. Afghanistan was plainly the focus when the authorization was enacted in September 2001, but the AUMF authorized the use of necessary and appropriate force against the organizations and persons connected to the September 11th attacks — al Qaeda and the Taliban — without a geographic limitation.

The legal point is important because, in fact, over the last 10 years al Qaeda has not only become more decentralized, it has also, for the most part, migrated away from Afghanistan to other places where it can find safe haven.

However, this legal conclusion too has its limits. It should not be interpreted to mean that we believe we are in any "Global War on Terror," or that we can use military force whenever we want, wherever we want. International legal principles, including respect for a state's sovereignty and the laws of war, impose important limits on our ability to act unilaterally, and on the way in which we can use force in foreign territories. . . .

[NSL p. 892, CTL p. 506. Insert at end of chapter.]

National Defense Authorization Act for Fiscal Year 2012

Pub. L. No. 112–81, 125 Stat. 1298, 1562-1564 (2011)

§1021. Affirmation of Authority of the Armed Forces of the United States to Detain Covered Persons Pursuant to the Authorization for Use of Military Force.

(a) In General. — Congress affirms that the authority of the President to use all necessary and appropriate force pursuant to the Authorization for Use of Military Force (Public Law 107–40; 50 U.S.C. 1541 note) includes the authority for the Armed Forces of the United States to detain covered persons (as defined in subsection (b)) pending disposition under the law of war.

(b) Covered Persons. — A covered person under this section is any person as follows:

(1) A person who planned, authorized, committed, or aided the terrorist attacks that occurred on September 11, 2001, or harbored those responsible for those attacks.

(2) A person who was a part of or substantially supported al-Qaeda, the Taliban, or associated forces that are engaged in hostilities against the United States or its coalition partners, including any person who has committed a belligerent act or has directly supported such hostilities in aid of such enemy forces.

(c) Disposition under Law of War. — The disposition of a person under the law of war as described in subsection (a) may include the following:

(1) Detention under the law of war without trial until the end of the hostilities authorized by the Authorization for Use of Military Force.

(2) Trial under chapter 47A of title 10, United States Code (as amended by the Military Commissions Act of 2009).

(3) Transfer for trial by an alternative court or competent tribunal having lawful jurisdiction.

(4) Transfer to the custody or control of the person's country of origin, any other foreign country, or any other foreign entity.

(d) Construction. — Nothing in this section is intended to limit or expand the authority of the President or the scope of the Authorization for Use of Military Force.

(e) Authorities. — Nothing in this section shall be construed to affect existing law or authorities relating to the detention of United States citizens, lawful resident aliens of the United States, or any other persons who are captured or arrested in the United States. . . .

§1022. Military Custody for Foreign Al-qaeda Terrorists.

(a) Custody Pending Disposition under Law of War. —

(1) In General. — Except as provided in paragraph (4), the Armed Forces of the United States shall hold a person described in paragraph (2) who is captured in the course of hostilities authorized by the Authorization for Use of Military Force (Public Law 107–40) in military custody pending disposition under the law of war.

(2) Covered Persons. — The requirement in paragraph (1) shall apply to any person whose detention is authorized under section 1021 who is determined —

(A) to be a member of, or part of, al-Qaeda or an associated force that acts in coordination with or pursuant to the direction of al-Qaeda; and

(B) to have participated in the course of planning or carrying out an attack or attempted attack against the United States or its coalition partners.

(3) Disposition under Law of War. — For purposes of this subsection, the disposition of a person under the law of war has the meaning given in section 1021(c) . . . .

(4) Waiver for National Security. — The President may waive the requirement of paragraph (1) if the President submits to Congress a certification in writing that such a waiver is in the national security interests of the United States.

(b) Applicability to United States Citizens and Lawful Resident Aliens. —

(1) United States Citizens. — The requirement to detain a person in military custody under this section does not extend to citizens of the United States.

(2) Lawful Resident Aliens. — The requirement to detain a person in military custody under this section does not extend to a lawful resident alien of the United States on the basis of conduct taking place within the United States, except to the extent permitted

by the Constitution of the United States.

(c) Implementation Procedures. — . . .

   (2) . . .

       (B) . . . [T]he requirement for military custody under
   subsection (a)(1) does not require the interruption of ongoing
   surveillance or intelligence gathering with regard to persons not
   already in the custody or control of the United States.

       (C) . . . [A] determination under subsection (a)(2) is not
   required to be implemented until after the conclusion of an
   interrogation which is ongoing at the time the determination is
   made and does not require the interruption of any such ongoing
   interrogation. . . .

(d) Authorities. — Nothing in this section shall be construed to
affect the existing criminal enforcement and national security authorities
of the Federal Bureau of Investigation or any other domestic law
enforcement agency with regard to a covered person, regardless whether
such covered person is held in military custody. . . .

Statement by the President on H.R. 1540

Dec. 31, 2011

Today I have signed into law H.R. 1540, the "National Defense
Authorization Act for Fiscal Year 2012." . . .

. . . I have signed this bill despite having serious reservations with
certain provisions that regulate the detention, interrogation, and
prosecution of suspected terrorists. . . .

Section 1021 affirms the executive branch's authority to detain
persons covered by the 2001 Authorization for Use of Military Force
(AUMF) (Public Law 107-40; 50 U.S.C. 1541 note). This section breaks
no new ground and is unnecessary. The authority it describes was
included in the 2001 AUMF, as recognized by the Supreme Court and
confirmed through lower court decisions since then. . . . I want to clarify
that my Administration will not authorize the indefinite military
detention without trial of American citizens. . . .

Section 1022 seeks to require military custody for a narrow category
of non-citizen detainees who are "captured in the course of hostilities
authorized by the Authorization for Use of Military Force." This section
is ill-conceived and will do nothing to improve the security of the United

States. The executive branch already has the authority to detain in
military custody those members of al-Qa'ida who are captured in the
course of hostilities authorized by the AUMF, and as Commander in
Chief I have directed the military to do so where appropriate. I reject any
approach that would mandate military custody where law enforcement
provides the best method of incapacitating a terrorist threat. While
section 1022 is unnecessary and has the potential to create uncertainty, I
have signed the bill because I believe that this section can be interpreted
and applied in a manner that avoids undue harm to our current
operations. . . .

. . . [U]nder no circumstances will my Administration accept or
adhere to a rigid across-the-board requirement for military detention. . . .

Barack Obama

Presidential Policy Directive/PPD-14 — Requirements of the National Defense Authorization Act
Feb. 28, 2012

SUBJECT: Procedures Implementing Section 1022 of the National
        Defense Authorization Act for Fiscal Year (FY) 2012

. . .

A rigid, inflexible requirement to place suspected terrorists into
military custody would undermine the national security interests of the
United States, compromising our ability to collect intelligence and to
incapacitate dangerous individuals. This Directive specifies policies and
procedures designed to ensure that section 1022 of the NDAA is
implemented in a manner that is consistent with the national security and
foreign policy interests of the United States. . . .

II. WAIVERS TO PROTECT NATIONAL
SECURITY INTERESTS ...

B. Protection of U.S. National Security Interests. In accordance with section 1022(a)(4) of the NDAA, and consistent with section 1022(c)(2), which provides the executive branch with broad discretion to design implementing procedures to ensure that the requirements of section 1022 do not interfere with various authorities necessary to disrupt or respond to terrorism threats, and to ensure that counterterrorism professionals have clear guidance and appropriate tools at their disposal to accomplish their mission effectively, I hereby waive the requirements of section 1022(a)(1), regardless of whether an individual has yet been determined to be a Covered Person, and certify that it is in the national security interests of the United States to do so, when:

> placing a foreign country's nationals or residents in U.S. military custody will impede counterterrorism cooperation, including but not limited to sharing intelligence or providing other cooperation or assistance to the United States in investigations or prosecutions of suspected terrorists;

> a foreign government indicates that it will not extradite or consent to the transfer of individuals to the United States if such individuals may be placed in military custody;

> an individual is a lawful permanent resident of the United States who is arrested inside the United States or is arrested by a Federal agency on the basis of conduct taking place in the United States, to the extent the individual is subject to the requirement of section 1022(a)(1);

> an individual has been arrested by a Federal agency in the United States on charges other than terrorism offenses (unless such individual is subsequently charged with one or more terrorism offenses and held in Federal custody in connection with those offenses);

> an individual has been arrested by State or local law enforcement, pursuant to State or local authority, and is transferred to Federal custody;

> transferring an individual to U.S. military custody could interfere with efforts to secure an individual's cooperation or confession; or

> transferring an individual to U.S. military custody could interfere with efforts to conduct joint trials with co-defendants who are ineligible for U.S. military custody or as to whom a determination has already been made to proceed with a prosecution in a Federal or State court.

C. Authority to Issue Additional Categorical National Security Waivers. The Attorney General, in consultation with other senior national security officials, shall have authority to waive the requirements of section 1022(a)(1) of the NDAA in the national security interests of the United States for categories of conduct or categories of individuals consistent with section 1022(a)(4).

     D. Authority to Issue Individual National Security Waivers. The Attorney General, in consultation with other senior national security officials, shall have the authority to waive the requirements of section 1022(a)(1) of the NDAA in the national security interests of the United States on an individual, case-by-case basis, consistent with section 1022(a)(4). A decision to issue such a waiver shall take into account factors such as: the legal and evidentiary strength of any criminal charges that may be brought against the individual; the likely punishment if convicted; the impact on intelligence collection of maintaining the individual in law enforcement custody; the legal and investigative risks posed by a transfer to U.S. military custody; the effect any transfer to U.S. military custody would likely have on cooperation by the individual in custody; the effect any transfer to U.S. military custody would likely have on cooperation by foreign governments in a particular investigation or related investigations; the risk associated with litigation concerning the legal authority to detain the individual pursuant to the 2001 AUMF, as informed by the laws of war; and the need to preserve a long-term disposition of the individual that adequately mitigates the threat the individual poses and protects the national security interests of the United States. A waiver is also appropriate if the Attorney General determines, in consultation with other senior national security officials, that a prosecution of the individual in Federal, State, or a foreign court will best protect the national security interests of the United States. . . .

III. LAW ENFORCEMENT ARRESTS OF INDIVIDUALS BELIEVED TO BE COVERED PERSONS . . .

     B. Screening. For each individual in [the custody of the FBI or other federal law enforcement agency], a screening shall commence as soon as practicable after sufficient information is available, in the estimation of the Attorney General, to establish that probable cause exists to believe that the individual is a Covered Person and that the individual is not currently subject to a National Security Waiver. . . .

C. Process for Making Covered Person Determinations. . . .

No further action shall be required under section 1022(a)(1) of the NDAA or the procedures set out in this Directive if the Attorney General, in coordination with other senior national security officials,

> determines that there is not clear and convincing evidence that such individual is a Covered Person;
> determines that such individual is subject to a categorical National Security Waiver specified in section II(B) or issued pursuant to section II(C) of this Directive; or
> issues an individual National Security Waiver under section II(D) of this Directive. . . .

F. Effect of Covered Person Determination. A determination that an individual is a Covered Person not subject to a National Security Waiver shall be without prejudice to that individual's appropriate disposition under the law of war in accordance with sections 1021(c) and 1022(a)(3) of the NDAA, the national security and foreign policy interests of the United States, and the interests of justice. . . .

V. NO ABRIDGMENT OF DOMESTIC LAW ENFORCEMENT

. . . After a Covered Person determination is made and implemented, the Department of Justice and the FBI shall retain lead responsibility for coordinating the investigation, including interrogation, while the Covered Person is held in military custody pending disposition under the law of war. . . .

Hedges v. Obama

United States District Court, Southern District of New York, 2012
2012 WL 1721124

KATHERINE B. FORREST, District Judge. On December 31, 2011, President Obama signed into law the National Defense Authorization Act for Fiscal Year 2012, Pub. L. 112–81, 125 Stat. 1298 (Dec. 31, 2011) (the "NDAA"). Plaintiffs, a group of writers and activists, brought a lawsuit on January 13, 2012, seeking preliminary and permanent injunctive relief with respect to one section (indeed, one page) of that voluminous legislation: §1021. Plaintiffs assert that Section 1021 is constitutionally infirm, violating both their free speech and associational rights guaranteed by the First Amendment as well as due process rights guaranteed by the Fifth Amendment of the United States Constitution. . . .

. . . The Government opposes plaintiffs' request for preliminary injunctive relief on three bases: first, that plaintiffs lack standing; second, that even if they have standing, they have failed to demonstrate an imminent threat requiring preliminary relief; and finally, through a series of arguments that counter plaintiffs' substantive constitutional challenges, that Section 1021 of the NDAA is simply an "affirmation" or "reaffirmation" of the authority conferred by the 2001 Authorization for Use of Military Force, Pub. L. 107–40, 115 Stat. 224 (Sept. 18, 2011) (the "AUMF"), passed in the wake of September 11, 2001.

In essence, the Government argues that as an "affirmation" of the AUMF, §1021 of the NDAA does nothing new; and therefore, since the type of activities in which plaintiffs are engaged were not subject to legal action under the AUMF, there is no reasonable basis for plaintiffs to assert that §1021 could suddenly subject them to governmental action now. . . .

BACKGROUND

I. The Statutes . . .

A. The AUMF . . .

President Bush utilized the authorization granted under the AUMF to send U.S. armed forces into Afghanistan "with a mission to subdue al Qaeda and quell the Taliban regime that was known to support it." *Hamdi v. Rumsfeld,* 542 U.S. 507, 510 (2004) (plurality); *accord Rasul v. Bush,* 542 U.S. 466, 470 (2004). The hostilities that commenced in 2001 remain ongoing today. The Government has captured and detained a number of individuals pursuant to the authority in the AUMF. *See generally, e.g., Hamdi,* 542 U.S. 507.

In *Hamdi,* the Supreme Court recognized the authority granted by the AUMF to detain the individuals captured: "detention of individuals . . . for the duration of the particular conflict in which they were captured, is so fundamental and accepted an incident to war as to be an exercise of the 'necessary and appropriate force' Congress has authorized the President to use." *Id.* at 518. . . .

B. The NDAA . . .

[Here the court sets out relevant parts of §1021 of the NDAA.] . . .

II. The Parties

A. Plaintiffs . . .

1. Christopher Hedges

At the hearing in this matter, Hedges testified that he has been a foreign correspondent for 20 years. He won the Pulitzer Prize for journalistic reporting. Over the course of his career, he has primarily worked in Latin America, Africa, the Middle East, and the Balkans. He makes his living writing, teaching, and lecturing. He has published a number of articles in the New York Times, the Christian Science Monitor, the Dallas Morning News, Harper's Magazine, and the New York Review of Books.

After September 11, 2001, Hedges was based in Paris and covered al-Qaeda in all European countries (with the exception of Germany) as well as the Middle East. As part of that coverage, Hedges retraced the steps of Mohammed Atta, one of the participants in the 9/11 events; he covered the abortive Paris embassy bombing plot, the suicide bombing attack on the synagogue in Djerba in Tunisia, and he covered Richard Reed, the so-called "Shoe Bomber."

Hedges testified that some of the people he has interviewed in connection with his work were al-Qaeda members who were later detained and are currently in prison. Accordingly to Hedges himself, his reporting on al-Qaeda or other terrorist organizations is read widely in the Middle East. Certain of Hedges' writings appear on Islamic or jihadist websites. . . .

Hedges testified that he has read §1021 of the NDAA. Hedges testified that he is also familiar with the provisions of the AUMF and has a specific understanding as to what they mean. He does not, however, understand that §1021 is entirely co-extensive and goes no further than the AUMF. Indeed, he testified that he reads §1021 as "radically different" from the AUMF. In that regard, Hedges is unclear as to the meaning of what constitutes "associated forces" in §1021, nor does he understand what the phrases "engaged in hostilities," "covered person," or "substantially supported" means as used in §1021.

Hedges testified that he has reported on 17 groups contained on a list prepared by the State Department of known terrorist organizations. . . .

Other groups Hedges has covered, such as the Popular Front for the Liberation of Palestine ("PFLP"), have carried out acts of terrorism against U.S. targets.

Hedges has also had a number of speaking engagements in Belgium and France in which he has encountered and conversed with members of al-Qaeda and the Taliban. . . .

Hedges testified that because he speaks a number of languages, he has been approached by publications — *e.g.,* Harper's Magazine, the Nation and others — to return to the Middle East as a correspondent. He testified that he has a realistic expectation that his work will bring him back to the Middle East.

Hedges testified that since the passage of §1021, he has altered his associational and speech activities with respect to some of the organizations upon which he previously reported due to his concern that those activities might bring him within the ambit of §1021, thereby subjecting him to indefinite military detention. *See, e.g .,* Tr. 174, 177, 186 ("When people begin to speak about carrying out acts that are clearly illegal or embracing acts that are violent or talking about terrorism, my reaction so far is to get out as fast as I can because I think under the NDAA [*i.e.,* §1021], at least as I see it, there is a possibility that those people looking at my activities from the outside would not make a distinction between myself and the person who embraced that kind of activity."). At the time of the hearing, Hedges had speeches scheduled in Paris and Brussels at which he expected members of al-Qaeda or the Taliban to be present and he intended to change his speech as a result of §1021. . . .

[Here the court describes the testimony of three other plaintiffs, to the same general effect.]

III. The Government's Representations Regarding §1021 . . .

The Court asked whether there was any language in the AUMF similar to §1021(b)(2) regarding in particular the phrases "substantially supported," "associated forces," and "directly supported." . . . [Conceding that no court had yet construed either of the first two terms,] the Government argued that the phrase "associated forces" can be tied directly into the body of law relating to the Laws of War as being co-extensive with co-belligerency. According to the Government, therefore, the Laws of War place important and clear limits on which organizations can be construed as "associated forces." . . .

The Court then asked: Give me an example. Tell me what it means to substantially support associated forces.

Government: I'm not in a position to give specific examples.

Court: Give me one.

Government: I'm not in a position to give one specific example.

The Court then asked: What does "directly supported" mean?

Government: We have not said anything about that in our brief.

Court: What do you think it means?

Government: . . . Your Honor, we had focused so much on the phrase that was challenged by the plaintiffs, "substantial support" that I have not thought through exactly and we have not come to a position on what "direct support" and what that means.

The Court then asked: "Assume you were just an American citizen and you're reading the statute and you wanted to make sure you do not run afoul of it because you are a diligent U.S. citizen wanting to stay on the right side of §1021, and you read the phrase 'directly supported.' What does that mean to you?"

Government: Again it has to be taken in the context of armed conflict informed by the laws of war.

Court: That's fine. Tell me what that means?

The Government then returned to the Laws of War and finally stated, "I cannot offer a specific example. I don't have a specific example."

The Court then asked the Government specific questions regarding plaintiffs' present and intended activities at issue here and whether those activities would fall within the scope of §1021. . . . [T]he Government responded, "I can't make specific representations as to particular plaintiffs. I can't give particular people a promise of anything."

It must be said that it would have been a rather simple matter for the Government to have stated that as to these plaintiffs and the conduct as to which they would testify, that §1021 did not and would not apply, if indeed it did or would not. That could have eliminated the standing of these plaintiffs and their claims of irreparable harm. Failure to be able to make such a representation given the prior notice of the activities at issue requires this Court to assume that, in fact, the Government takes the position that a wide swath of expressive and associational conduct is in fact encompassed by §1021. . . .

DISCUSSION . . .

I. Article III and Plaintiffs' Standing

Article III, § 2 of the United States Constitution empowers this Court only to entertain actual cases and controversies. "Standing doctrine determines 'whether the plaintiff has made out a 'case or controversy' between himself and the defendant within the meaning of Art. III' and is therefore 'entitled to have the courts decide the merits of the dispute or of particular issues.'" *Amnesty Int'l USA v. Clapper,* 638 F.3d 118, 131 (2d Cir. 2011) (quoting *Warth v. Seldin,* 422 U.S. 490, 498 (1975)). "A citizen who dislikes a particular law may not require a court to address its constitutionality simply by stating in a complaint his belief, however deeply held, that the law is inconsistent with some provision of the Constitution." *Id.* Concrete injury is required. *Id.* . . .

Here, each of the four plaintiffs who testified . . . has shown an actual fear that their expressive and associational activities are covered by §1021; and each of them has put forward uncontroverted evidence of concrete — non-hypothetical — ways in which the presence of the legislation has already impacted those expressive and associational activities.

For instance, Hedges has testified that he is currently concerned about associating with certain individuals and in fact has now removed himself from certain situations in the course of his professional activities because of that concern. In addition, given his prior journalistic activities relating to certain organizations such as al-Qaeda and the Taliban, as well as others that are denominated terrorist organizations by the U.S.

State Department (*e.g.,* associating with these individuals in these groups as part of his investigative work, reporting on the groups in the press), he has a realistic fear that those activities will subject him to detention under §1021. That fear cannot be said to be ill-founded when, at the injunction hearing itself, the Government was unwilling to commit that such conduct does not fall within §1021's ambit. . . .

Further, with respect to the "costs" undertaken to avoid being prosecuted under the challenged statute . . . , the Court finds that all four plaintiffs have sufficiently sustained "costs" to confer standing. The Court does not find that the costs incurred must be monetary. . . . The costs to plaintiffs in changing their respective associational or expressive activities imposes concrete, personal, human costs on these plaintiffs. Forgoing professional opportunities cannot be said not to carry some costs, even of those costs cannot be quantified in monetary terms. The human costs associated with altering their behavior — both in their personal, day-to-day lives as well as their professional lives — are certainly cognizable costs undertaken based upon their reasonable fear. . . .

. . . [T]he injunctive relief requested by plaintiffs will, at least preliminarily, redress the alleged injuries connected to enactment of §1021. . . .

Accordingly, [the four plaintiffs who testified in court] have sufficiently established their standing to bring this action.

II. Plaintiffs' Motion for Preliminary Injunction

In order for plaintiffs to demonstrate entitlement to preliminary injunctive relief, they must demonstrate (a) a likelihood of success on the merits of their claims of constitutional infirmity; (b) that they will suffer irreparable harm in the absence of the requested relief; (c) that the balance of the equities tips in their favor; and (d) that the injunction is in the public interest. *Winter v. Natural Resources Defense Council,* 555 U.S. 7, 20 (2008). . . .

1. Likelihood Of Success On The Merits . . .

a. Facial versus As Applied Challenge: The First Amendment

This Court approaches plaintiffs' facial challenge to §1021 with great caution. The Supreme Court has repeatedly cautioned that facial challenges to the constitutionality of a law — which, if successful, would invalidate the entirety of the law — are disfavored. *Washington State Grange v. Washington State Republican Party,* 552 U.S. 442, 449 (2008). Outside the context of the First Amendment, it is accepted that a facial challenge must generally fail when a statute has a plainly legitimate sweep. *Id.* . . .

The statute at issue here has a plainly legitimate sweep. Indeed, as this Court noted at the evidentiary hearing, the conduct in which the plaintiffs here engage is without a doubt *not* the core conduct that is intended to be covered by the statute. Section 1021 is a statute aimed at individuals associating with, and providing some degree of support (a degree known only to the drafters of §1021, if at all), terrorists connected to al-Qaeda and the Taliban. It stands to reason that the type of person Congress intended to be "covered" under §1021 is someone who has taken up arms, or might be providing arms, to al-Qaeda, the Taliban or some of their off-shoots. No doubt the public should be protected from such people and we should affirmatively defer to Congress and those in appropriate law enforcement and military positions wherever possible as to how best to accomplish this.

Nevertheless, with respect to §1021, and particularly in light of the Government's representations that it could not represent that plaintiffs' expressive and associational conduct does not bring them within the ambit of the statute, plaintiffs have stated a more than plausible claim that the statute inappropriately encroaches on their rights under the First Amendment. . . .

. . . "[W]here the statute unquestionably attaches sanctions to protected conduct [e.g., expressive and associational conduct], the likelihood that the statute will deter that conduct is ordinarily sufficiently great to justify an overbreadth attack." *Erznoznik v. City of Jacksonville,* 422 U.S. 205, 217 (1975). . . .

A facial challenge is appropriate here. . . .

b.   Likelihood of Success on Plaintiffs' First Amendment Claim

Here, each of the four plaintiffs who testified at the evidentiary hearing put forward evidence that their expressive and associational conduct has been and will continue to be chilled by §1021. The Government was unable or unwilling to represent that such conduct was not encompassed within §1021. Plaintiffs have therefore put forward uncontroverted proof of infringement on their First Amendment rights.

Applying strict scrutiny to the question of whether there is a compelling government interest that outweighs infringement upon First Amendment rights, the Court finds that plaintiffs have shown a likelihood of success that there is not. Again, that is particularly so in light of the Government's position that §1021 does no more than the AUMF; therefore, the infringing potential for §1021 may well be unintentional, but it is real nonetheless. There is no doubt that the type of speech in which [the plaintiffs] engage is political in nature. It is also likely that some of their views may be extreme and unpopular as measured against views of an average individual. That, however, is precisely what the First Amendment protects. . . .

. . . [T]his Court finds that plaintiffs have shown a likelihood of succeeding on the merits of a facial challenge to §1021.

c. The Due Process Challenge: Is the Statute Void for Vagueness?

To satisfy the Due Process Clause of the Fifth Amendment, individuals are entitled to understand the scope and nature of statutes which might subject them to criminal penalties. Thus, "[a] penal statute must define the criminal offense (1) with sufficient definiteness that ordinary people can understand what conduct is prohibited and (2) in a manner that does not encourage arbitrary and discriminatory enforcement." *Skilling v. United States,* 130 S. Ct. 2896, 2928 (2010). That analysis is performed against the backdrop of a strong presumption of validity given to acts of Congress. *Id.* . . .

. . . [T]here is an exception to the general rule that vagueness challenges are generally evaluated on an "as applied" basis: courts have allowed facial attacks for vagueness when a criminal statute lacks a *mens rea* requirement, even in the absence of an accompanying First Amendment challenge. *See City of Chicago v. Morales,* 527 U.S. 41 (1999). . . . [Section] 1021 (unlike §1022, or even 18 U.S.C. §§2339A/B — *i.e.,* the statute(s) under review in *Holder* [*v. Humanitarian Law Project,* 130 S. Ct. 2705 (2010)]) lacks a knowledge requirement; an individual could fall within the definition of "covered person" under §1021 without having either intentionally or recklessly known that he or she was doing so.

A question, then, for this Court is whether §1021 should be treated as analogous to a criminal statute. If it is, then the test set forth in *Skilling* applies. . . . [T]his Court preliminarily finds that §1021, which could be used for the indeterminate military detention, is sufficiently akin to a criminal statute to be treated as such. At the hearing on this motion, the Government was unwilling or unable to state that these plaintiffs would not be subject to indefinite detention under §1021. Plaintiffs are therefore at risk of detention, of losing their liberty, potentially for many years. In relevant part, then, that is the analytical equivalent of a penal statute.

Before anyone should be subjected to the possibility of indefinite military detention, the Due Process Clause of the Fifth Amendment requires that individuals be able to understand what conduct might cause him or her to run afoul of §1021. Unfortunately, there are a number of terms that are sufficiently vague that no ordinary citizen can reliably define such conduct. . . .

The Government's strongest position is with respect to the definition of "associated forces." The Government argued that there is an accepted definition of what constitutes "associated force" under the Laws of War, which is defined in terms of principles of co-belligerency and the Laws of War. Specifically, "associated forces" is understood, at least by the Government, to be "'individuals who, in analogous circumstances in a traditional international armed conflict between the armed forces of opposing governments, would be detainable under principles of co-belligerency.'" The Court notes that even accepting the Government's definition of "associated forces," that does not resolve plaintiffs' concerns since they each testified to activities with or involving individuals or organizations that are "associated forces" as defined by the Government.

As to "substantially" or "direct" "support," plaintiffs have the stronger argument, stating that those terms lack sufficient definition. That is particularly persuasive in light of the fact that a number of other statutes, including the prong of the NDAA that directly follows this one (*i.e.,* §1022 of the NDAA), have lengthy definitional provisions. The Government was unable to define precisely what "direct" or "substantial" "support" means. Instead, the Government pointed to cases in which the phrase "substantially supported" had been referred to in connection with the interpretation of the AUMF, but also conceded, as it must, that the parameters of "substantial support" were not at issue and not addressed in those cases. In addition, the Government conceded that the statute lacks a scienter or mens rea requirement of any kind. Thus, an individual could run the risk of substantially supporting or directly supporting an associated force without even being aware that he or she was doing so.

Finally, and most importantly of course, the Government was unable to state that plaintiffs' conduct fell outside §1021. In the face of what could be indeterminate military detention, due process requires more. Indeed, §1022 of the NDAA contains a long series of definitions, as [do] 18 U.S.C. §§ 2339A and 2339B (examined in *Holder*). In *Holder,* the Supreme Court specifically found that the statute at issue was not unconstitutionally vague because of the very definitions and the knowledge requirement that are missing from this statute. *See Holder,* 130 S. Ct. at 2719-22.

. . . The vagueness of §1021 does not allow the average citizen, or even the Government itself, to understand with the type of definiteness to which our citizens are entitled, or what conduct comes within its scope. . . .

2. *Irreparable Injury*

The second essential element of sustaining a claim for preliminary injunctive relief is that a plaintiff suffers irreparable harm in the absence of such relief. *Salinger* [*v. Colting,* 607 F.3d 68 (2d Cir. 2010),] at 80. In the context of the First Amendment, the Supreme Court has held that the loss of First Amendment freedoms, for even minimal periods of time, unquestionably constitutes irreparable injury. *Elrod v. Burns,* 427 U.S. 347, 373 (1976). . . .

Here, the uncontradicted testimony at the evidentiary hearing was that the plaintiffs have in fact lost certain First Amendment freedoms as a result of the enactment of §1021. [Three of the plaintiffs] have changed certain associational conduct, and [two plaintiffs] have avoided certain expressive conduct, because of their concerns about §1021. Under *Elrod* and *Salinger,* that is sufficient to meet the element of irreparable harm. Moreover, since plaintiffs continue to have their associational and expressive conduct chilled, there is both actual and continued threatened irreparable harm.

In addition, it is certainly the case that if plaintiffs were detained as a result of their conduct, they could be detained until the cessation of hostilities — *i.e.,* an indeterminate period of time. Being subjected to the risk of such detention, particularly in light of the Government's inability to represent that plaintiffs' conduct does not fall with §1021, must constitute a threat of irreparable harm. The question then is: Is that harm immediate? Since the Government will not say that the conduct does not fall outside of §1021, one cannot predict immediacy one way or the other. . . .

The Government argues that there cannot be a threat of imminent harm because §1021 is simply an "affirmation" of the AUMF — and since plaintiffs have not to date been subject to detention under the AUMF, there is no reasonable basis for them to fear detention under §1021. That argument, however, ignores that . . . there are obvious differences between the AUMF and §1021. Section 1021 is certainly far from a verbatim reprise of the AUMF. This Court assumes, as it must, that Congress acted intentionally when crafting the differences as between the two statutes.

First, by its terms, the AUMF is tied directly and only to those involved in the events of 9/11. Pub. L. 107-40, 115 Stat. 224 at §2(a) (authorization of the president to use force related to "attacks that occurred on September 11, 2001). Section 1021, in contrast, has a non-specific definition of "covered person" that reaches beyond those involved in the 9/11 attacks by its very terms. To wit, §1021 speaks in terms of "engaged in hostilities," id.; that is the present progressive tense, not the past tense relating to 9/11.

Relatedly, the individuals or groups at issue in the AUMF are also more specific than those at issue in §1021. At issue in the AUMF are those who were directly involved in the 9/11 attacks while those in §1021 are specific groups and "associated forces." But the Government has not provided a concrete, cognizable set of organizations or individuals that constitute "associated forces," lending further indefiniteness to §1021.

Further, any question of "support" is specifically defined by the verbs in the statute — i.e., "planned," "authorized," "committed," or "aided" in relation to the 9/11 attacks themselves or "harbored" in relation to the organizations or persons who engaged in the just-discussed acts. Pub. L. 107-40, 115 Stat. 224 at §2(a). Such clarity is not provided in §1021 with respect to what acts — and what mental state related to those acts — falls within the broad, general phrase of "substantial support."

Thus, the indefinite — indeed, vague — nature of §1021, coupled with the Government's inability to provide assurances that the specific conduct at issue here (of which the Government had ample notice) would not subject plaintiffs to prosecution and detention for their acts lays the foundation for plaintiffs' reasonable fear of irreparable harm.

3. Balancing Of The Equities

In considering whether to issue a preliminary injunction, the Court must consider, as noted above, "the balance of the hardships between the plaintiff and defendant and issue the injunction only if the balance of the hardships tips in the plaintiff's favor." *Salinger,* 607 F.3d at 80.

The Government's primary argument in opposition to this motion is that §1021 is simply an affirmation of the AUMF; that it goes no further, it does nothing more. . . . Thus, to the extent the Government believes that the two provisions are co-extensive, enjoining any action under §1021 should not have any impact on the Government.

Even if, however, §1021 does convey some authority not provided under the AUMF, the equities nonetheless tip strongly in favor of enjoining its enforcement. The Government was given a number of opportunities at the hearing and in its briefs to state unambiguously that the type of expressive and associational activities engaged in by plaintiffs — or others — are not within §1021. It did not. This Court therefore must credit the chilling impact on First Amendment rights as reasonable — and real. Given our society's strong commitment to protecting First Amendment rights, the equities must tip in favor of protecting those rights.

Moreover, Congress can add definitional language to the statute and resolve the issues the plaintiffs have raised and the Court has flagged. By adding definitions and imposing a scienter requirement, it can resolve the issues with the statute and proceed with enforcement activities it deems fit. In the meantime, there are a variety of other statutes which can be utilized to detain those engaged in various levels of support of terrorists — including the AUMF and §1022. Thus, preliminarily enjoining the enforcement of §1021 does not divest the Government of its many other tools.

4. Public Interest

There is a strong public interest in protecting rights guaranteed by the First Amendment. There is also a strong public interest in ensuring that due process rights guaranteed by the Fifth Amendment are protected by ensuring that ordinary citizens are able to understand the scope of conduct that could subject them to indefinite military detention.

Weighed against these public interests is the strong public interest in upholding acts of Congress and thereby maintaining the appropriate separation of powers; there is also a clear public interest which counsels for cautious use of judicial power to enjoin an act of Congress, and the public interest in ensuring protection from terroristic acts — and that law enforcement has the tools necessary to be as effective as possible in that regard.

The Government has assisted the Court in its deliberations with respect to the risks associated with the various interests on each side of the ledger. In light of the Government's contention that §1021 does nothing new, that it goes no further than the AUMF, the Court can only assume that the Government believes that preliminarily enjoining enforcement of §1021 will not expose the public to any increased risk and that §1021 does not add anything new to law enforcement's tools.

This Court is acutely aware that preliminarily enjoining an act of Congress must be done with great caution. However, it is the responsibility of our judicial system to protect the public from acts of Congress which infringe upon constitutional rights. As set forth above, this Court has found that plaintiffs have shown a likelihood of success on the merits regarding their constitutional claim and it therefore has a responsibility to insure that the public's constitutional rights are protected.

Accordingly, this Court finds that the public interest is best served by the issuance of the preliminary relief recited herein.

CONCLUSION

For the aforementioned reasons, plaintiffs' motion for preliminary injunction is GRANTED; enforcement of §1021 of the NDAA is preliminarily enjoined pending further order of this Court or amendments to the statute rendering this Opinion & Order moot. . . .

So Ordered.

———————————

[NSL p. 951, CTL p. 565. Insert at end of chapter.]

Padilla v. Yoo
United States Court of Appeals, Ninth Circuit, 2012
678 F.3d 748

FISHER, Circuit Judge: After the September 11, 2001 attacks on the United States, the government detained Jose Padilla, an American citizen, as an enemy combatant. Padilla alleges that he was held incommunicado in military detention, subjected to coercive interrogation techniques and detained under harsh conditions of confinement, all in violation of his constitutional and statutory rights. In this lawsuit, plaintiffs Padilla and his mother, Estela Lebron, seek to hold defendant John Yoo, who was the Deputy Assistant Attorney General in the U.S. Department of Justice's Office of Legal Counsel (OLC) from 2001 to 2003, liable for damages they allege they suffered from these unlawful actions. Under recent Supreme Court law, however, we are compelled to conclude that, regardless of the legality of Padilla's detention and the wisdom of Yoo's judgments, at the time he acted the law was not "sufficiently clear that every reasonable official would have understood that what he [wa]s doing violate[d]" the plaintiffs' rights. We therefore hold that Yoo must be granted qualified immunity, and accordingly reverse the decision of the district court.

As we explain below, we reach this conclusion for two reasons. First, although during Yoo's tenure at OLC the constitutional rights of convicted prisoners and persons subject to ordinary criminal process were, in many respects, clearly established, it was not "beyond debate" at that time that Padilla — who was not a convicted prisoner or criminal defendant, but a suspected terrorist designated an enemy combatant and confined to military detention by order of the President — was entitled to the same constitutional protections as an ordinary convicted prisoner or accused criminal. Second, although it has been clearly established for decades that torture of an American citizen violates the Constitution, and we assume without deciding that Padilla's alleged treatment rose to the level of torture, that such treatment *was* torture was not clearly established in 2001-03.

I. BACKGROUND

A. . . .

[For the background of Padilla's initial arrest, military detention, and subsequent transfer to civilian custody, see NSL pp. 855-857 or CTL pp. 469-471.]

Padilla and his mother, Estela Lebron, filed this civil action against John Yoo, in his individual capacity, on January 4, 2008, two years after Padilla's military detention ended. . . . Padilla and Lebron alleged that Padilla was imprisoned in the military brig without charge and without the ability to defend himself or to challenge his conditions of confinement. They alleged that during Padilla's detention, he suffered gross physical and psychological abuse upon the orders of high-ranking government officials as part of a systematic program of abusive interrogation mirroring the alleged abuses committed at Guantanamo Bay, including extreme isolation; interrogation under threat of torture, deportation and even death; prolonged sleep adjustment and sensory deprivation; exposure to extreme temperatures and noxious odors; denial of access to necessary medical and psychiatric care; substantial interference with his ability to practice his religion; and incommunicado detention for almost two years, without access to family, counsel or the courts. . . .

. . . From 2001 to 2003, Yoo was Deputy Assistant Attorney General at OLC. Padilla and Lebron alleged that Yoo set in motion Padilla's allegedly illegal interrogation and detention, both by formulating unlawful policies for the designation, detention and interrogation of suspected "enemy combatants" and by issuing legal memoranda designed to evade legal restraints on those policies and to immunize those who implemented them. They alleged that, in doing so, Yoo abdicated his ethical duties as a government attorney and abandoned his office's tradition of providing objective legal advice to the President.

The complaint alleged that Yoo publicly acknowledged in his book, *War By Other Means,* that he stepped beyond his role as a lawyer to participate directly in developing policy in the war on terrorism. It alleged that Yoo shaped government policy in his role as a key member of a small, secretive and highly influential group of senior administration officials known as the "War Council," which met regularly "to develop policy in the war on terrorism." It alleged that Yoo acted outside the scope of his employment at OLC by taking instructions directly from White House Counsel Alberto Gonzales and providing Gonzales with verbal and written advice without first consulting Attorney General John Ashcroft. The complaint alleged that, in his role as the de facto head of war-on-terrorism legal issues, Yoo wrote and promulgated a series of memoranda that ultimately led to Padilla's allegedly unlawful treatment . . . .

The complaint alleged that these memoranda advised that there were no legal constraints on the Executive's policies with respect to the detention and interrogation of suspected terrorists. It alleged that the memoranda "did not provide the fair and impartial evaluation of the law required by OLC tradition and the ethical obligations of an attorney to provide the client with an exposition of the law adequate to make an informed decision." Rather, it alleged that Yoo "intentionally used the Memos to evade well-established legal constraints and to justify illegal policy choices that he knew had already been made — sometimes by virtue of his own participation in the War Council."

The complaint also alleged that Yoo personally participated in Padilla's unlawful military detention. Quoting from Yoo's book, it alleged that Yoo "personally 'reviewed the material on Padilla to determine whether he could qualify, legally, as an enemy combatant, and issued an opinion to that effect.'" It alleged that Ashcroft relied on Yoo's opinion in recommending to the President that Padilla be taken into military custody.

The complaint alleged that Padilla's designation as an enemy combatant, military detention, conditions of confinement and program of interrogation violated his rights to procedural and substantive due process, not to be subjected to cruel or unusual punishment or treatment that shocks the conscience, to freely exercise his religion, of access to information, to association with family members and friends, of access to legal counsel, of access to the courts, against compelled self-incrimination and against arbitrary and unconstitutional seizure and military detention. It alleged violations of the First, Fourth, Fifth, Sixth and Eighth Amendments to the United States Constitution, Article III of the Constitution, the Habeas Suspension and Treason Clauses of the Constitution and the Religious Freedom Restoration Act (RFRA), 42 U.S.C. §2000bb. . . .

B.

Yoo moved to dismiss the action for failure to state a claim upon which relief could be granted. He argued that the complaint failed to state a claim for money damages on three grounds. First, he argued that

the plaintiffs could not state an action for damages because *Bivens* . . .
did not apply. [In *Lebron v. Rumsfeld*, 670 F.3d 540 (4th Cir. 2012), the
Fourth Circuit relied on this argument in dismissing Padilla's damages
suit against those military and law enforcement officials directly
involved in his detention and alleged mistreatment]. Second, Yoo argued
that he was entitled to qualified immunity because the complaint failed
to allege facts sufficient to establish his personal responsibility for the
constitutional and statutory violations alleged in the complaint. Third,
Yoo argued that he was entitled to qualified immunity because the
complaint failed to allege a violation of clearly established constitutional
or statutory rights. . . .

II. DISCUSSION

A.

The outcome of this appeal is governed by the Supreme Court's
decision in *Ashcroft v. al-Kidd,* 131 S. Ct. 2074 (2011) [NSL p. 754;
CTL p. 368]. . . .

The Court [in *al-Kidd*] began by reaffirming the general principle
that "[q]ualified immunity shields federal and state officials from money
damages unless a plaintiff pleads facts showing (1) that the official
violated a statutory or constitutional right, and (2) that the right was
'clearly established' at the time of the challenged conduct." *Id.* at 2080.
Significant here, under the second prong, a "Government official's
conduct violates clearly established law when, at the time of the
challenged conduct, '[t]he contours of [a] right [are] sufficiently clear'
that every 'reasonable official would have understood that what he is
doing violates that right.'" *Id.* at 2083. "We do not require a case directly
on point, but existing precedent must have placed the statutory or
constitutional question beyond debate." *Id.* The Court emphasized that
"[q]ualified immunity gives government officials breathing room to
make reasonable but mistaken judgments about open legal questions,"
id. at 2085, and admonished us "not to define clearly established law at a
high level of generality." *Id.* at 2084. . . .

Here, the complaint alleged that Yoo, as a Justice Department
attorney, participated in policy decisions and rendered legal opinions
that ultimately authorized federal officials to designate Padilla as an
enemy combatant, take him into military custody, hold him
incommunicado without access to the courts or counsel and subject him

to both coercive interrogation techniques and harsh conditions of confinement, in violation of his constitutional and statutory rights.

Padilla and Lebron acknowledge that at the time Yoo served as Deputy Assistant Attorney General at OLC, there did not exist a "single judicial opinion," holding that a United States citizen held in military detention as an enemy combatant possessed rights against the kind of treatment to which Padilla was subjected. They argue, however, that it was clearly established that Padilla possessed such rights because any reasonable official would have understood during 2001 to 2003 that a citizen detained as an enemy combatant had to be afforded at least the constitutional protections to which convicted prisoners and ordinary criminal suspects were entitled. That argument is foreclosed by *al-Kidd*, which compels us "not to define clearly established law at a high level of generality." . . .

Here, of course, the Supreme Court had not, at the time of Yoo's tenure at OLC, declared that American citizens detained as enemy combatants had to be treated at least as well, or afforded at least the same constitutional and statutory protections, as convicted prisoners. On the contrary, the Supreme Court had suggested in *Ex parte Quirin*, 317 U.S. 1 (1942), the most germane precedent in existence at the time of Yoo's tenure at OLC, that a citizen detained as an unlawful combatant could be afforded *lesser* rights than ordinary prisoners or individuals in ordinary criminal proceedings. . . .

Padilla and Lebron alternatively rely on the Supreme Court's decision in *Hamdi v. Rumsfeld*, 542 U.S. 507 (2004) [NSL p. 831, CTL p. 445], to establish that Padilla's treatment violated clearly established law. . . . When measured against [at least some of the] language in *Hamdi*, Padilla's alleged cruel and degrading treatment appears to have been a violation of his constitutional rights.

Hamdi, however, was not decided until 2004, so it could not have placed Yoo on clear notice of Padilla's constitutional rights in 2001-03 when Yoo was at the Department of Justice. Even after *Hamdi*, moreover, it remains murky whether an enemy combatant detainee may be subjected to conditions of confinement and methods of interrogation that would be unconstitutional if applied in the ordinary prison and criminal settings. Although *Hamdi* recognized that citizens detained as enemy combatants retain constitutional rights to due process, the Court suggested that those rights may not be coextensive with those enjoyed by other kinds of detainees. On the contrary, the Court held that the rights afforded to an enemy combatant detainee "may be tailored" to the circumstances, because "the full protections that accompany challenges to detentions in other settings may prove unworkable and inappropriate in the enemy-combatant setting." *Id.* at 535.

In sum, the plaintiffs did not, through their reliance on either *Hamdi* or cases involving ordinary prison and criminal settings, allege violations of constitutional and statutory rights that were clearly established in 2001-03. During that relevant time frame, the constitutional rights of convicted prisoners and persons subject to *ordinary* criminal process were, in many respects, clearly established. But Padilla was not a convicted prisoner or criminal defendant; he was a suspected terrorist designated an enemy combatant and confined to military detention by order of the President. He was detained as such because, in the opinion of the President — albeit allegedly informed by his subordinates, including Yoo — Padilla presented a grave danger to national security and possessed valuable intelligence information that, if communicated to the United States, could have been helpful to the United States in staving off further terrorist attacks. We express no opinion as to whether those allegations were true, or whether, even if true, they justified the extreme conditions of confinement to which Padilla says he was subjected. In light of Padilla's status as a designated enemy combatant, however, we cannot agree with the plaintiffs that he was just another detainee — or that it would necessarily have been "apparent" to someone in Yoo's position that Padilla was entitled to the same constitutional protections as an ordinary convicted prisoner or accused criminal. Given the unique circumstances and purposes of Padilla's detention, and in light of *Quirin,* an official could have had some reason to believe that Padilla's harsh treatment fell within constitutional bounds. . . .

B.

The absence of a decision defining the constitutional and statutory rights of citizens detained as enemy combatants need not be fatal to the plaintiffs' claims. The Supreme Court has long held that "officials can still be on notice that their conduct violates established law even in novel factual circumstances." *Hope v. Pelzer,* 536 U.S. 730, 741 (2002).

The plaintiffs invoke this principle here. They argue that, even if there is no specific judicial decision holding that the Fifth Amendment's prohibition on government conduct that "shocks the conscience" is violated when the government tortures a United States citizen designated as an enemy combatant, torture of a United States citizen is the kind of egregious constitutional violation for which a decision "directly on point" is not required. We agree with the plaintiffs that the unconstitutionality of torturing a United States citizen was "beyond debate" by 2001.[9] Yoo is entitled to qualified immunity, however, because it was not clearly established in 2001-03 that the treatment to which Padilla says he was subjected amounted to torture.

In 2001-03, there was general agreement that torture meant the intentional infliction of severe pain or suffering, whether physical or mental. The meaning of "severe pain or suffering," however, was less clear in 2001-03. *See, e.g.*, Michael W. Lewis, *A Dark Descent into Reality: Making the Case for an Objective Definition of Torture*, 67 Wash. & Lee L. Rev. 77, 82-83 (2010); Judith Resnik, *Detention, the War on Terror, and the Federal Courts*, 110 Colum. L. Rev. 579, 633-34 (2010); Sanford Levinson, *In Quest of a "Common Conscience": Reflections on the Current Debate About Torture*, 1 J. Nat'l Security L. & Pol'y 231, 231-52 (2005).

In several influential judicial decisions in existence at the time of Yoo's tenure at OLC, for example, courts had declined to define certain severe interrogation techniques as torture:

Ireland v. United Kingdom, 25 Eur. Ct. H.R. (ser. A) (1978), is the European Court of Human Rights' leading decision on torture. The court considered whether five interrogation techniques used by the United Kingdom to interrogate suspected members of the Irish Republican Army violated Article 3 of the European Convention of Human Rights, which prohibits both torture and "inhuman or degrading treatment or punishment." The five techniques at issue were wall standing (i.e., stress positions), hooding, subjection to noise, sleep deprivation and deprivation of food and drink. . . . The court concluded that "[a]lthough the five techniques, as applied in combination, undoubtedly amounted to inhuman and degrading treatment," in violation of Article 3, "they did not occasion suffering of the particular intensity and cruelty implied by the word torture as so understood." *Id.* at 80.

In *HCJ 5100/94 Public Committee Against Torture in Israel v. Israel* 53(4) PD 817 [1999] (Isr.), the Israeli Supreme Court considered

---

9. That substantive due process under the Fifth Amendment prohibits the government from engaging in conduct that "shocks the conscience" has long been clearly established. What has not been clearly established is how that standard applies to citizens detained as enemy combatants.

whether coercive techniques used by Israeli security forces violated international law. The techniques included hooding, violent shaking, painful stress positions, exposure to loud music and sleep deprivation. The court concluded that each of these techniques was illegal, although the court did not address whether they constituted torture rather than cruel, inhuman and degrading treatment, which was also prohibited by international law.

In *Price v. Socialist People's Libyan Arab Jamahiriya*, 294 F.3d 82 (D.C. Cir. 2002), the plaintiffs were two American citizens imprisoned in Libya, allegedly for political reasons. They alleged that they endured deplorable conditions while incarcerated, including urine-soaked mattresses, a cramped cell with substandard plumbing they were forced to share with seven other inmates, a lack of medical care and inadequate food. They also alleged that they were "kicked, clubbed and beaten" by prison guards, and "interrogated and subjected to physical, mental and verbal abuse." The plaintiffs sued Libya under the Foreign Sovereign Immunities Act, alleging torture. The court held that the plaintiffs had failed to adequately allege torture because they did not allege sufficiently *severe* pain or suffering, noting that "[t]he critical issue is the degree of pain and suffering that the alleged torturer intended to, and actually did, inflict upon the victim. The more intense, lasting, or heinous the agony, the more likely it is to be torture." *Id.* at 93. Although the plaintiffs alleged that they suffered "kicking, clubbing, and beatings," there was "no way to determine from the present complaint the severity of plaintiffs' alleged beatings — including their frequency, duration, the parts of the body at which they were aimed, and the weapons used to carry them out." *Id.*

In other decisions in existence at the time of Yoo's OLC tenure, this Circuit found torture, but the treatment at issue was more severe than that to which Padilla was allegedly subjected:

In *Al-Saher v. INS*, 268 F.3d 1143 (9th Cir. 2001), *amended on another ground*, 355 F.3d 1140 (9th Cir. 2004), an immigration case, we concluded that the petitioner was entitled to relief under the Convention Against Torture and Other Cruel, Inhuman or Degrading Treatment or Punishment (CAT) because he had been tortured in Iraq. On one occasion, the petitioner was detained, interrogated and severely beaten for one month. During his interrogations, he was blindfolded and his hands were tied behind his back. On another occasion, he was blindfolded, restrained, beaten and burned with cigarettes over an 8- to 10-day period. Noting that these actions "were specifically intended by officials to inflict severe physical pain" on the petitioner, we held, under CAT, that he suffered torture. *Id.* at 1147-48.

In *Hilao v. Estate of Marcos*, 103 F.3d 789 (9th Cir. 1996), an Alien Tort Statute case, we held that two plaintiffs, Sison and Piopongco, were tortured in the Philippines during the regime of Ferdinand Marcos. Sison had been interrogated by members of the military, who blindfolded and severely beat him while he was handcuffed and fettered; threatened him with electric shock and death; denied him sleep; and imprisoned him for seven months in a suffocatingly hot and unlit cell, measuring 2.5 meters square, during which time he was shackled to his cot, his handcuffs often so tight that the slightest movement made them cut into his flesh. During this period, Sison felt "extreme" and "almost undescribable" pain. After his seven months shackled to his cot, Sison spent more than eight years in detention, approximately five of them in solitary confinement and the rest in near-solitary confinement. In one round of interrogation, lasting six hours, Sison's limbs were shackled to a cot, a towel was placed over his nose and mouth and his interrogators then poured water down his nostrils so that he felt as though he were drowning. The other plaintiff — Piopongco — was arrested, held incommunicado, interrogated, subjected to mock executions and threatened with death.

Here, Padilla alleged that he was subjected to prolonged isolation; deprivation of light; exposure to prolonged periods of light and darkness, including being "periodically subjected to absolute light or darkness for periods in excess of twenty-four hours"; extreme variations in temperature; sleep adjustment; threats of severe physical abuse; death threats; administration of psychotropic drugs; shackling and manacling for hours at a time; use of "stress" positions; noxious fumes that caused pain to eyes and nose; loud noises; withholding of any mattress, pillow, sheet or blanket; forced grooming; suspensions of showers; removal of religious items; constant surveillance; incommunicado detention, including denial of all contact with family and legal counsel for a 21-month period; interference with religious observance; and denial of medical care for "serious and potentially life-threatening ailments, including chest pain and difficulty breathing, as well as for treatment of the chronic, extreme pain caused by being forced to endure stress positions." The complaint also alleged, albeit in conclusory fashion, that Padilla "suffered and continues to suffer severe mental and physical harm as a result of the forty-four months of unlawful military detention and interrogation." It also alleged that Padilla suffered "severe physical pain" and "profound disruption of his senses and personality."

We assume without deciding that Padilla's alleged treatment rose to the level of torture. That it *was* torture was not, however, "beyond debate" in 2001-03. There was at that time considerable debate, both in and out of government, over the definition of torture as applied to specific interrogation techniques. In light of that debate, as well as the judicial decisions discussed above, we cannot say that any reasonable official in 2001-03 would have known that the specific interrogation techniques allegedly employed against Padilla, however appalling, necessarily amounted to torture. Thus, although we hold that the unconstitutionality of torturing an American citizen was beyond debate in 2001-03, it was not clearly established at that time that the treatment Padilla alleges he was subjected to amounted to torture.

C.

For these reasons, we hold that Yoo is entitled to qualified immunity on the plaintiffs' claims.[16] Because we reverse on that basis, we do not address Yoo's alternative arguments that the complaint does not adequately allege his personal responsibility for Padilla's treatment and that a *Bivens* remedy is unavailable.

Our conclusion that Yoo is entitled to qualified immunity does not address the propriety of Yoo's performance of his duties at OLC otherwise. As amici point out, the complaint alleges that Yoo "*intentionally* violated professional standards reflected in OLC practice and *willfully* disregarded the obligations attendant on his office." Amici argue that "[s]uch conduct, if proven, would strike at the very heart of OLC's mission and seriously compromise the ability of the executive to make informed, even lawful, decisions." These allegations have been the subject of an internal Department of Justice investigation of Yoo's compliance with professional standards and are not at issue here.

---

16. We have discretion to decide which of the two prongs of qualified immunity analysis to address first. *See al-Kidd*, 131 S. Ct. at 2080 (citing *Pearson v. Callahan*, 555 U.S. 223, 236 (2009)). Here, we consider only the second prong.

III. CONCLUSION

Yoo is entitled to qualified immunity. The order of the district court denying Yoo's motion to dismiss is therefore reversed in pertinent part.

Reversed.

NOTES AND QUESTIONS

1. *"Clearly Established" Law.* In *Harlow v. Fitzgerald*, 457 U.S. 800 (1982), the Supreme Court articulated the modern standard for qualified immunity. Under *Harlow*, "government officials performing discretionary functions generally are shielded from liability for civil damages insofar as their conduct does not violate clearly established statutory or constitutional rights of which a reasonable person would have known." Thus, damages suits like *Padilla* raise two different questions: the "illegality" question (whether the plaintiff's rights actually *were* violated) and the "liability" question (whether the defendant officer should have known that his conduct violated the plaintiff's "clearly established" rights). Do you see why the plaintiff must prevail on both questions in order to recover, whereas the defendant prevails if either question is resolved in his favor?

2. *Torture vs. CIDT.* Given the *Harlow* standard, what did the Ninth Circuit actually hold in *Padilla*? Did the Court of Appeals decide that Padilla's alleged mistreatment did or did not constitute torture? That it did or did not constitute cruel, inhuman, or degrading treatment (CIDT)? Why does the torture/CIDT distinction seem to matter so much to the Court of Appeals? Was it clear from 2001 to 2003 that torture was prohibited by U.S. law? Was it clear during the same time period that CIDT was unlawful? Was it clear during that time period on which side of the torture/CIDT line Padilla's alleged mistreatment fell? Is it clear today?

3. *The Specificity of the Legal Claim.* In *Padilla*, the court notes the Supreme Court's decision in *Hope v. Pelzer*, 536 U.S. 730 (2002), which rejected the argument that a defendant is entitled to qualified immunity unless the individual right at issue has been clearly established by a prior case squarely on point both legally *and* factually. Instead, *Hope* framed the inquiry as asking whether "in the light of pre-existing law the

unlawfulness [should have been] apparent." 536 U.S. at 739. Given that standard, are you convinced by the *Padilla* court's analysis of prior case law, including the foreign and international decisions discussed earlier? After *Hope*, is the question whether Padilla's alleged mistreatment was as bad as that suffered by the plaintiffs in those cases, or rather whether those cases *should have* established the unlawfulness of the measures that were allegedly authorized against Padilla? Is this a distinction worth a difference?

4. *Footnote 16 and the Order of Battle.* In its decision in *Saucier v. Katz*, 533 U.S. 194 (2001), the Supreme Court mandated an "order of battle" in qualified immunity cases, pursuant to which courts had to first decide the illegality question before turning to the liability question. The justification for such an approach was to ensure that, even in cases in which the unlawfulness of the defendant's conduct was *not* clearly established (where the defendant therefore prevailed on liability), the law *would be* established going forward. Lower-court judges, who were often left to decide constitutional questions that were not necessary to the result, complained bitterly, leading the Supreme Court to abandon the "*Saucier* sequence" in *Pearson v. Callahan*, 555 U.S. 223 (2009). Under *Pearson*, courts *may*, but need not, resolve the illegality question in cases in which the law was not clearly established. In footnote 16, the *Padilla* court cites *Pearson* to explain why it can sidestep whether Padilla's rights were *actually* violated. Do you see why *Padilla* will therefore have virtually no precedential effect? *Should* the Ninth Circuit have decided whether, going forward, Padilla's alleged mistreatment actually *was* a violation of his rights?

5. *National Security Litigation and the Pearson Problem.* Many damages suits against government officers arise out of conduct that can be challenged through other forms of litigation, including suits for prospective relief while the allegedly unlawful conduct is occurring, or as defenses to criminal prosecutions. In those contexts, *Pearson*'s effect on law-formation may not be significant, since judges will have numerous chances to articulate forward-looking principles of constitutional law in similar cases. But the same may not be true in national security litigation, given the far smaller number of putative victims, the uniqueness of many of the claims in such cases, and the government's prosecutorial discretion. Indeed, as the *Padilla* litigation itself demonstrates, the government will often take affirmative steps to

avoid a judicial decision on the merits in national security cases. One of us has suggested that "the general rule articulated in *Pearson* will wreak particular havoc in the national security context, potentially freezing (or, at a minimum, substantially slowing) the development of constitutional law with regard to the surveillance, detention, and treatment of terrorism suspects." Stephen I. Vladeck, *The New National Security Canon*, 61 Am. U. L. Rev. 1295, 1328 (2012). If so, and if this is a problem worth a solution, should courts in cases like *Padilla* feel impelled to decide the illegality question even if they are not required to do so? Is there a better solution to this "*Pearson* problem"?

[NSL p. 1113, CTL p. 727. Insert at end of chapter.]

Eric Holder, Attorney General, Remarks at Northwestern University School of Law
Mar. 5, 2012,
available at
http://www.justice.gov/iso/opa/ag/speeches/2012/ag-speech-1203051.html

. . .

It's important to note that the reformed [military] commissions draw from the same fundamental protections of a fair trial that underlie our civilian courts. They provide a presumption of innocence and require proof of guilt beyond a reasonable doubt. They afford the accused the right to counsel — as well as the right to present evidence and cross-examine witnesses. They prohibit the use of statements obtained through torture or cruel, inhuman, or degrading treatment. And they secure the right to appeal to Article III judges — all the way to the United States Supreme Court. In addition, like our federal civilian courts, reformed commissions allow for the protection of sensitive sources and methods of intelligence gathering, and for the safety and security of participants.

A key difference is that, in military commissions, evidentiary rules reflect the realities of the battlefield and of conducting investigations in a war zone. For example, statements may be admissible even in the absence of Miranda warnings, because we cannot expect military personnel to administer warnings to an enemy captured in battle. But instead, a military judge must make other findings — for instance, that the statement is reliable and that it was made voluntarily.

I have faith in the framework and promise of our military commissions, which is why I've sent several cases to the reformed commissions for prosecution. There is, quite simply, no inherent contradiction between using military commissions in appropriate cases while still prosecuting other terrorists in civilian courts. Without question, there are differences between these systems that must be — and will continue to be — weighed carefully. Such decisions about how to prosecute suspected terrorists are core Executive Branch functions. In each case, prosecutors and counterterrorism professionals across the government conduct an intensive review of case-specific facts designed to determine which avenue of prosecution to pursue.

Several practical considerations affect the choice of forum.

First of all, the commissions only have jurisdiction to prosecute individuals who are a part of al Qaeda, have engaged in hostilities against the United States or its coalition partners, or who have purposefully and materially supported such hostilities. This means that there may be members of certain terrorist groups who fall outside the jurisdiction of military commissions because, for example, they lack ties to al Qaeda and their conduct does not otherwise make them subject to prosecution in this forum. Additionally, by statute, military commissions cannot be used to try U.S. citizens.

Second, our civilian courts cover a much broader set of offenses than the military commissions, which can only prosecute specified offenses, including violations of the laws of war and other offenses traditionally triable by military commission. This means federal prosecutors have a wider range of tools that can be used to incapacitate suspected terrorists. Those charges, and the sentences they carry upon successful conviction, can provide important incentives to reach plea agreements and convince defendants to cooperate with federal authorities.

Third, there is the issue of international cooperation. A number of countries have indicated that they will not cooperate with the United States in certain counterterrorism efforts — for instance, in providing evidence or extraditing suspects — if we intend to use that cooperation in pursuit of a military commission prosecution. Although the use of military commissions in the United States can be traced back to the early days of our nation, in their present form they are less familiar to the international community than our time-tested criminal justice system and Article III courts. However, it is my hope that, with time and experience, the reformed commissions will attain similar respect in the eyes of the world. . . .

And we will continue to reject the false idea that we must choose between federal courts and military commissions, instead of using them both. If we were to fail to use all necessary and available tools at our disposal, we would undoubtedly fail in our fundamental duty to protect the Nation and its people. That is simply not an outcome we can accept. . . .

* * *